THE ULTIMATE GUIDE TO
WINNING

Brand Crossword Game

Michael Lawrence
and
John Ozag

BANTAM BOOKS
TORONTO • NEW YORK • LONDON • SYDNEY • AUCKLAND

This is book is dedicated to
all of you who have ever wondered what to do
when you get FHIJKUZ or AMTTTUW on your Scrabble® racks.
Here is the answer.

THE ULTIMATE GUIDE TO WINNING SCRABBLE® BRAND CROSSWORD GAME
A Bantam Book / August 1987

Library of Congress Cataloging-in-Publication Data

Lawrence, Mike.
The ultimate guide to winning Scrabble® brand crossword game.

1. Scrabble (Game)   I. Ozag, John.   II. Title.
GV1507.S3L38   1987   793.73   86-47570
ISBN 0-553-34306-8

Published simultaneously in the United States and Canada

PRINTED IN THE UNITED STATES OF AMERICA

BP   0 9 8 7 6 5 4 3 2 1

ACKNOWLEDGMENTS

Without the help of the following people, this book would never have progressed beyond the idea we had three years ago. Each in their own way has contributed to the publication of this book.

We would like to thank Bantam Books, Inc., and particularly our editor Peter Guzzardi. His support and enthusiasm was especially welcome during the long hours of editing and writing. Thanks also to Alison Acker, Barbara Cohen, Frances Nuelle, Richard Oriolo, and Donna Ruvituso for their cooperation and assistance.

Jim Houle, President of Scrabble® Players, Inc., was a vital link in putting this project together. His assistance in completing the contract with Selchow & Righter is greatly appreciated.

For creative ideas and proof reading, we want to thank Joe Edley, the 1980 national Scrabble® champion, as well as Robert Felt and Stu Goldman. Finally, we would like to thank each other: Mike for his vast experience as a games teacher, writer, and world-class games competitor; and John for his Scrabble® expertise, organization and tireless editing.

CONTENTS

SECTION THREE
(Games)

FOREWORD

When John Ozag, one of my favorite people and a fine Scrabble® player, told me that he was going to write a beginners' Scrabble® book with Mike Lawrence, one of the grand masters of bridge, someone I barely knew, and who knew little about Scrabble® *at the time*, I was somewhat surprised. (Hearing it over the phone and in the privacy of my apartment, no one could see my bulging eyes or the way I effortlessly tossed a head of broccoli onto the next block.) I knew that John's knowledge of the game was quite substantial. I had no doubts about his technical ability—but could he communicate his knowledge?

In the coming months I became good friends with Mike and learned through reading his books and talking to him just how exquisite a communicator he is. As the book was being shaped I heard from John about the long sessions where Mike, starting only with an insatiable curiosity about the game, would ask him a thousand questions about various aspects of Scrabble®, and John would patiently explain the details slowly and methodically, until Mike could express the ideas in his own brilliant style.

When they both asked me to read the final copy I was flat-out stunned! This book is a master blend of their two talents. The clarity with which each idea is presented will allow any reader of the English language the pleasure of learning, enjoying, and improving their skills at a game that has been steadily gaining participation from people the world over. I highly recommend dipping into the book anywhere and reading for yourself.

Whether you want to know *how* to look for the best plays or which tiles to keep, or which are the most important words to know, or would like to see examples of good strategy at work—here is the source that will give it to you. Well done, guys!

Joe Edley
1980 North American Scrabble® Champion

RULES

Perhaps because it permits so much variety, Scrabble®
is the most popular of all word games. A crossword-style game best
played by two people, Scrabble® is also entertaining with four players,
or even solitaire. The game consists of forming interlocking words in
crossword fashion on a playing board using letter tiles with various
score values. Words are scored by counting up the points of letters
used, adding in the effect of any premium squares. Each player
competes for high score by using his letters in combinations and
locations that take best advantage of letter values and premium
squares on the board. Play passes from person to person until all tiles
are used or until no more words can be formed. The winner is the
one who scores the most points. The combined total score for a game
may range from 500 to 900 points or more, based on the skill of the
players.

EQUIPMENT

Basic Scrabble® equipment consists of the board, which measures 15
squares by 15 squares, 100 letter tiles, and 4 racks, on which players
keep their tiles. Sand timers or a chess clock may be used to regulate
time. Squares on the board are of two basic types, premium and
nonpremium. There are 164 nonpremium squares (gray), 24 double-
letter-score squares (light blue), 17 double-word-score squares (pink),
12 triple-letter-score squares (dark blue), and 8 triple-word-score
squares (red). The center of the board, marked with a star, is also a
double-word-score square. It is specially marked because rules require
that one letter of the first word played must cover this square.

The number of tiles follows. As you'll see, there are far more tiles with
the letter E, for instance, than there are tiles with the letter Q, since E
is a very common letter, and Q quite rare.

A—9	F—2	K—1	P—2	U—4	Z—1
B—2	G—3	L—4	Q—1	V—2	*—2
C—2	H—2	M—2	R—6	W—2	
D—4	I—9	N—6	S—4	X—1	
E—12	J—1	O—8	T—6	Y—2	

The asterisk represents a blank tile that can be used for any letter a player wishes. It is a kind of joker, or wild card.

Each letter has a point value marked on the tile. The point value for each letter is:

A—1	F—4	K—5	P—3	U—1	Z—10
B—3	G—2	L—1	Q—10	V—4	*—0
C—3	H—4	M—3	R—1	W—4	
D—2	I—1	N—1	S—1	X—8	
E—1	J—8	O—1	T—1	Y—4	

Each letter rack holds seven tiles, the number that a player should have prior to each turn.

To START

After checking to see that all 100 tiles are present, place them face down either on the table, in the Scrabble® box, or in a deep cloth bag. Whichever method you use, the tiles must remain hidden until drawn from the pool and positioned on the board.

After shuffling the tiles thoroughly, each player draws one tile to determine who goes first. The player who draws the letter closest to A starts the game. If two players draw the same letter, they must redraw. If one player draws a blank it is considered the best tile and he starts even if another player draws an A. If two players draw blanks they must redraw. Additional players continue drawing to complete the order of play. The tiles are returned to the tile pool and reshuffled. The first player then chooses seven tiles and places them on his rack, not allowing his opponents to see them. Other players do the same.

The PLAY

Using two or more of his letters, the first player forms a word on the board either horizontally or vertically so that one letter of the word covers the center square (marked by a star). Horizontal words must be read from left to right and vertical words must be read from top to bottom. Diagonal words are not permitted. The score of the first play is the total of the values of the letters played plus the value of the double letter square if it is used, multiplied by 2 because the center star is a double-word-score square. (If you look at the board, you'll notice that in any direction you can reach only one double letter square, even if you use all seven letters for a bingo.) A player finishes his turn by announcing his score and taking as many tiles as necessary from the pool to give him seven on his rack. All players should keep a running score to minimize errors. As an alternative to playing a word, the first player may exchange tiles or, more rarely, pass in place. To do this, one must simply announce the pass or exchange and the number of tiles involved.

SUCCESSIVE MOVES

The second and subsequent players, each in turn, add one or more tiles to those already on the board to form one or more new words. All letters played in any single turn must be placed in one row across or down the board. At least one new letter must be placed adjacent to a letter already on the board. In this game, the first word played was HOUSE. Some examples:

1. Adding to the front of the word   OUTHOUSE at **8-A** (diagram 1)

2. Adding to the rear of the word   HOUSEBOY at **8-D** (diagram 2)

3. Adding to the front and the rear   UNHOUSED at **8-B** (diagram 3)

4. Playing vertically through a middle letter   ZERO at **E-5** (diagram 4)

5. Playing vertically through the first letter   CHARMS at **D-7** (diagram 5)

6. Playing vertically at the end of a word, changing its meaning   HARDY at **I-5** (diagram 6)

7. Playing horizontally above the word, forming three words   IMPLY at **7-G** (diagram 7)

8. Playing horizontally below the word, forming three words   THIN at **9-B** (diagram 8)

9. Playing horizontally below the word, forming four words   PORT at **9-F** (diagram 9)

LATER IN THE GAME

Further board development:

1. Horizontally, adding an S to an existing word   WORMS at **10-B** (diagram 10)

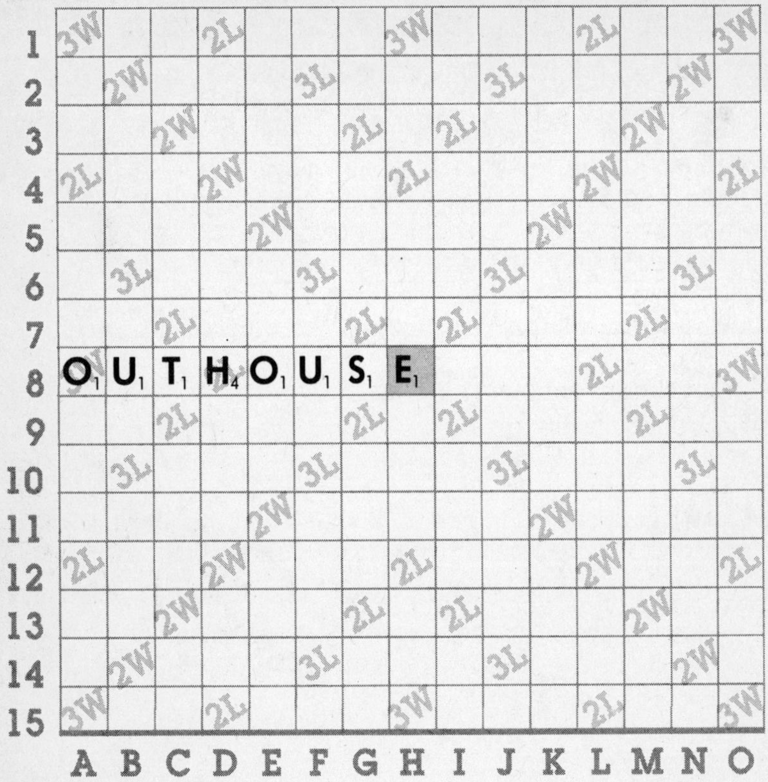

DIAGRAM 1

2. Horizontally, through two separated letters — HABIT at **4-C** (diagram 11)
3. Vertically, below an existing word — OH at **10-I** (diagram 12)
4. Vertically, through two joined letters — ENDURING at **H-8** (diagram 13)
5. Vertically, by adding an S — CLUMPS at **L-4** (diagram 14)

Notice that after the first word, no subsequent word may be played in isolation but must link with a word or words already played. A new word must form legal words at any intersection of letters it touches or face the possibility of a challenge. Once a turn is completed (the word positioned and the score announced), the letters may not be shifted.

DIAGRAM 2

DIAGRAM 3

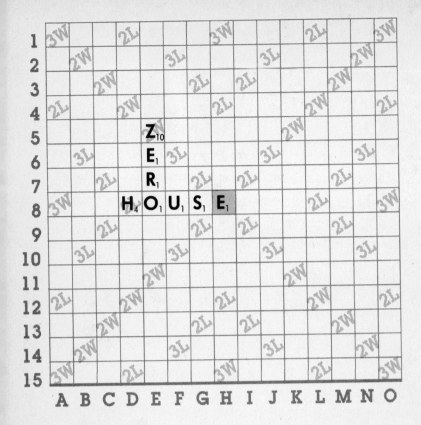

DIAGRAM 4

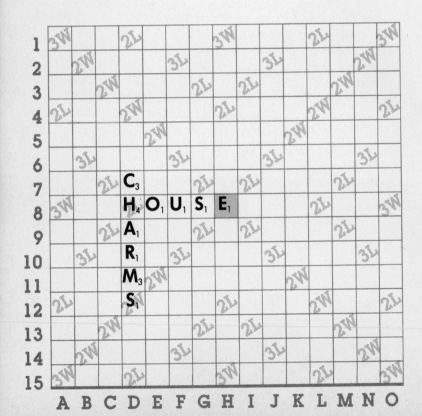

DIAGRAM 5

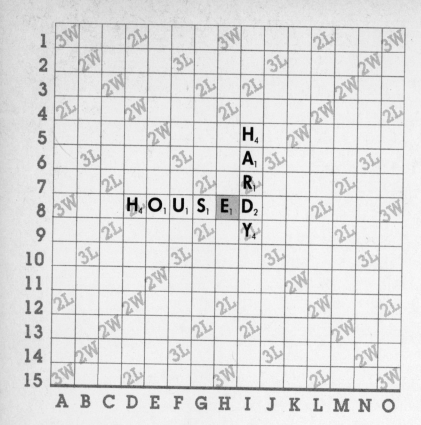

DIAGRAM 6

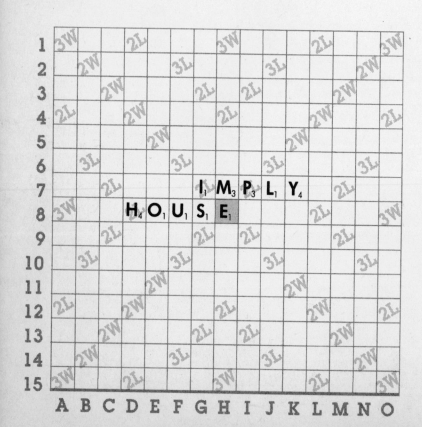

DIAGRAM 7

DIAGRAM 8

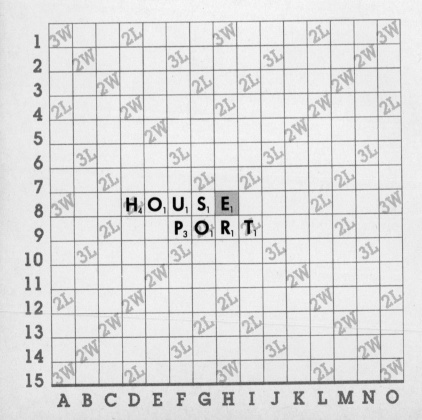

DIAGRAM 9

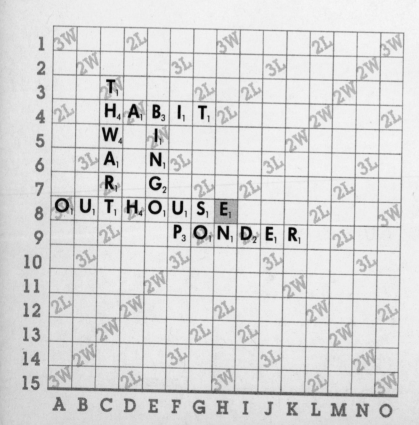

DIAGRAM 10

DIAGRAM 11

DIAGRAM 12

DIAGRAM 13

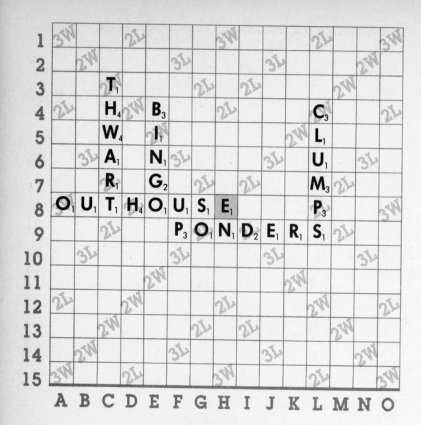

DIAGRAM 14

THE BLANK TILES

The blank tiles may be used to represent any letter desired. When a player uses a blank he should clearly state which letter it represents, after which it cannot be changed to represent any other letter during the course of the game. Each time a blank is placed on the board it is the responsibility of the opponent to turn the blank over to verify that it is truly a blank. If it is not a blank, the player who placed it on the board must take back all his tiles played during that turn and loses his turn. This is true even if the tile misplayed as a blank is the same letter as the bogus blank was supposed to be. If a false blank is not detected when it is placed on the board, it will remain on the board as a blank, and the game will continue with no penalty to either player.

EXCHANGING

Any player may use his turn to replace any or all of his tiles. So that you're sure not to get your own tiles back again in the exchange, first discard the unwanted tiles face down on the table, then draw the same number of new tiles. Once you are sure you have seven tiles in your rack again, mix the discarded tiles back into the pool. You may not play a new word as part of your turn. Exchanging may be done only as long as there are at least seven tiles in the pool.

Once there are fewer than seven tiles remaining, passing a turn without an exchange is permitted, but no exchanging is allowed. There are no limits on passing or exchanging during a game unless both players each pass a total of three consecutive turns—in which case the game is over.

OVERDRAWING

If a player draws too many tiles he must put all of his tiles on his rack and his opponent will remove and return to the pool all the excess tiles. This is done by a blind draw. However, the opponent has the right to see what these tiles are as he returns them to the pool.

WORDS

The *Official Scrabble® Players' Dictionary* (OSPD) is the accepted arbiter of all words with a base length of eight letters or less. For words with a base greater than eight letters, *Webster's Ninth New Collegiate Dictionary* is used. The dictionary or word lists may not be consulted during the game other than for challenges.

When a player completes his turn, his opponent may challenge any word or words that were formed during that play. This must be done before the next player begins his turn. If the challenged word is found unacceptable, the player who played it takes back his tiles and forfeits his turn. If the challenged word is ruled acceptable, the word remains and the challenger loses his turn. So, in a two-person game, the person playing the challenged word gets to play again. If the challenged play contains more than one word and any one word is ruled unacceptable, the challenge is successful and the person that played the word loses his turn. It is therefore important to note that when a given play is challenged, it benefits the challenger to challenge all words formed. If a phony word is not challenged, it stays on the board and is scored normally. The word can be challenged later only if it is modified. This is most often done by the addition of an S. In that case, the modifier rather than the original player bears full responsibility for the word.

Diagram 15 shows player 1 opening with NIPPY at **8-E**. Player 2 attempts the phony GRANOLA at **E-5**. It is not challenged. Thinking

DIAGRAM 15

that the word is acceptable, player 1 tries MISHAP at **12-C**. Player 2 challenges. MISHAP is allowable, GRANOLA(S) is not. Player 2 loses his turn for attempting to build on an invalid word.

Scoring

The score for each turn is the sum of the letter values in each word formed or modified during the play, plus any bonus points scored by using any of the premium squares.

PREMIUM LETTER SQUARES

1. A light blue square doubles the score of a letter placed on it. In PRY at **G-7**, diagram 16, multiply the value of the P by 2: $(3 \times 2) = 6$ and multiply the value of the Y by 2: $(4 \times 2) = 8$. Add 6 plus 8 plus 1 point for the R for a total of 15 points for the play.

2. A dark blue square triples the score of a letter placed on it. In FARM at **F-7**, diagram 17, multiply the value of the M by 3: $(3 \times 3) = 9$. Add this to the individual values of the F, A, and R $(9 + 4 + 1 + 1) = 15$ for the play.

DIAGRAM 16

DIAGRAM 17

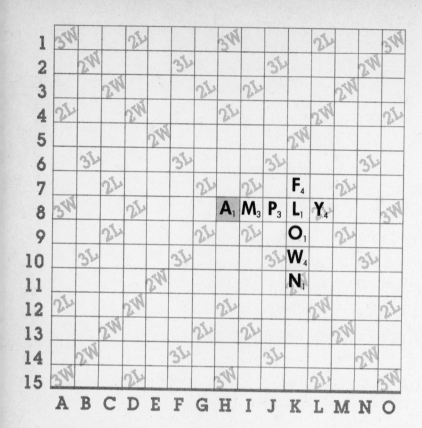

DIAGRAM 18

PREMIUM WORD SQUARES

1. The score for an entire word is doubled when one of the letters is placed on a pink square. In FLOWN at **K-7**, diagram 18, multiply the total value of the individual letters by 2: $(4 + 1 + 1 + 4 + 1) \times 2 = 22$ points total.

2. The score for an entire word is tripled when one of its letters is placed on a red square. In diagram 19 player 1 adds ING to DRINK at **8-H**. Add the total of the individual letters and multiply by 3: $(2 + 1 + 1 + 1 + 5 + 1 + 1 + 2) \times 3 = 42$ points.

3. Double or triple letter scores, if any, must be figured before doubling or tripling the word score. In diagram 20, adding DEATHS to HUT at **G-3**, triple the value of the H $(4 \times 3) = 12$, add that to the individual letter values of the other tiles, and multiply by 2: $((12) + (2 + 1 + 1 + 1 + 1)) \times 2 = 36$. Add to this the value for SHUT at **G-2** $(1 + 4 + 1 + 1) = 7$ for a total of 43.

DIAGRAM 19

DIAGRAM 20

DIAGRAM 21

Board (Diagram 21) letters:
- BOTHERS reading down column E: B$_3$ (E-5), O$_1$ (E-6), T$_1$ (E-7), H$_4$ (E-8), E$_1$ (E-9), R$_1$ (E-10), S$_1$ (E-11)
- HEMP reading across row 8: H$_4$ (E-8), E$_1$ (F-8), M$_3$ (G-8), P$_3$ (H-8)

4. Covering two double word squares gives you 4 times the total letter count. This is called a "double double." In BOTHERS at **E-5**, diagram 21, multiply the total of the individual letters by 4: $(3 + 1 + 1 + 4 + 1 + 1 + 1) \times 4 = 48$ points.

5. Covering two triple word squares gives you 9 times the total letter count. This is called a "triple triple." In MISCOUNT at **A-1**, diagram 22, multiply the total of the individual letters by 9 and add 50 for a bingo: $(3 + 1 + 1 + 3 + 1 + 1 + 1 + 1) \times 9 + 50 = 108 + 50 = 158$ points. (We'll explain bingos on p. 20)

6. Letter and word premiums are scored only on the original turn. In future turns these premiums do not apply. In JINGLE at **H-1**, diagram 23, score the triple word score but not the double letter score because it has already been used. It counts only as a regular square: $(8 + 1 + 1 + 2 + 1 + 1) \times 3 = 42$ points. Similarly with MINX at **1-A**, diagram 23, score the double letter score but not the triple word score. It has already been used. $(3 + 1 + 1) + (8 \times 2) = 21$ points.

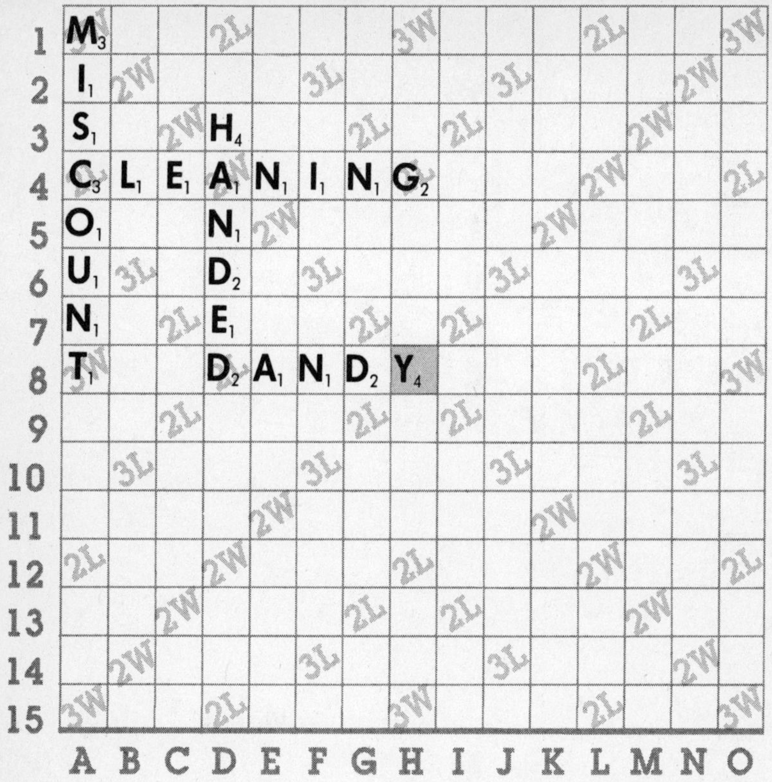

DIAGRAM 22

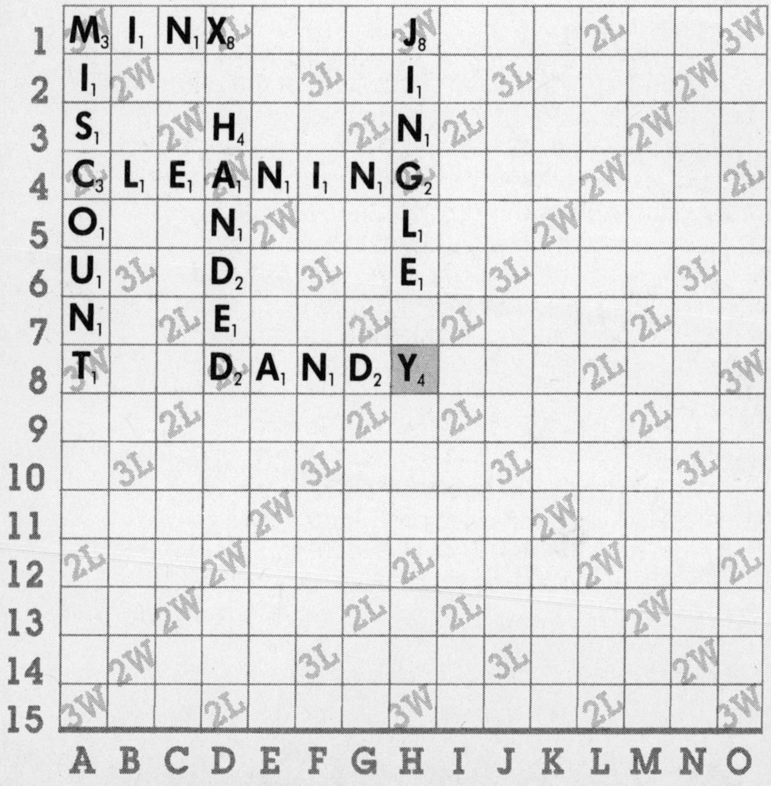

DIAGRAM 23

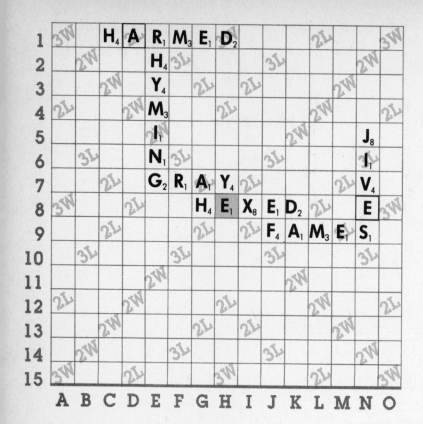

DIAGRAM 24

THE BLANK

The blank itself is worth zero points. However, if by using a blank a player is able to reach a premium word square, the sum of the other letters of the word is doubled or tripled, even though the blank has no numerical value. In diagram 24, both JIVES at **O-5** and HARMED at **1-D** utilize a blank that enables the player to reach the triple word square. Additionally, if by using a blank in any position a player is able to reach a premium letter square, the value of the particular letter is doubled or tripled. In diagram 25, both KAZOO at **6-H** and ADJOIN at **J-8** use a blank to take advantage of a triple letter score. Even though it has no point value itself, the blank then functions as a dynamic connector allowing a player to form bingos and utilize premium squares.

BINGOS

Whenever a player uses all seven tiles on one play he receives a bonus of 50 points. This is added after all other premiums have been computed. Diagram 26 shows how SHOOTER at **M-8** is scored. SHOOTER $(1 + (4 \times 2) + 1 + 1 + 1 + 1 + 1) \times 2 = 28$ points. Adding the S to CLANG at **8-H** gives us $3 + 1 + 1 + 1 + 2 + 1 = 9$ points. Combining the scores $28 + 9$ for the individual words and adding the 50-point bingo bonus totals 87 points. Diagram 26 indicates how the eight-letter

DIAGRAM 25

bingo OUTLAWED at **4-G** is scored. Tally the individual points: $1 + (2 \times 1) + 1 + 1 + 1 + 4 + 1 + 2 = 13$ points. Add 50 for the bingo for a total of 63 points. Note that you do not get the double word bonus, since this has already been used in WRONG at **L-4**.

THE END OF THE GAME

The game continues until all the tiles have been drawn and one player has used all of his tiles. Additionally, the game is over when neither player can form a word on the board.

If both players have unplayed tiles on their racks, each player's score is reduced by the sum of the point value of his unused tiles. For example, if player 1 has EEEO, add the points $1 + 1 + 1 + 1 = 4$ and subtract this from his score. If player 2 has FFL, add the points $4 + 4 + 1 = 9$ and subtract this from his score. On the other hand, if one player has used all his tiles, his score is increased by double the sum of his opponent's unplayed letters, and the opponent's score remains the same. For example, if player 2 was holding CDKO, add up the total points $(3 + 2 + 5 + 1 = 11)$, multiply by 2 $(11 \times 2 = 22)$, and add this amount to the score of player 1.

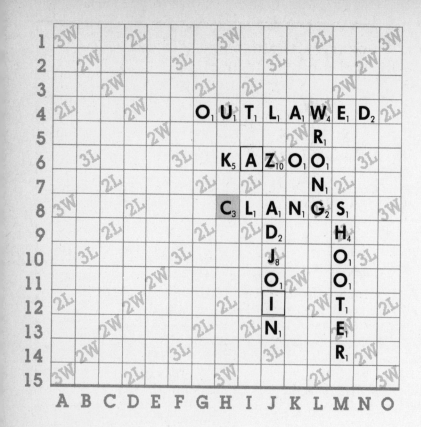

DIAGRAM 26

VARIATIONS

Variations from the official rules are allowed. To avoid confusion, all such changes should be clearly understood and agreed to by all players before the game begins.

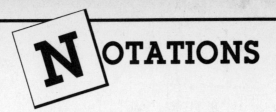

NOTATIONS

Since there will be frequent references to the Scrabble®
Crossword Game Board, a system of notation is needed. In 1975,
Selchow & Righter Company developed the "ABC/123 Notational
System" to identify the location of specific plays. This is an easy method
to use and has been widely adopted as the standard.*

The NUMBERS refer to the ROWS (across the page) and the LETTERS
refer to the COLUMNS (up and down the page).

Look at diagram 27. The first word played was UMP at **8-F**. The 8
indicates that UMP was played *horizontally* in the EIGHTH row and
that it started in the F column.

The second play was HUMID at **G-6**, diagram 28. The letter G indicates
that HUMID is played *vertically* in the G column, and the number 6
shows where the word starts. The *M* is italicized to indicate that it was
already on the board from an earlier play.

The third play consisted of adding the J to UMP, indicated by *JUMP* at
8-E, diagram 28.

The fourth play was DEFEN(D)ER at **10-G**. The second D has a box
around it, indicating that a blank tile was used. Diagram 28 shows
the position after DEFEN(D)ER is played.

When you see notations like these:

DUCK (ACT)   at **9-E**
VALUE (VY)   at **H-2**
PARKA (AI)   at **C-7**

the letters in parentheses are the letters remaining in your rack after
your play. These letters are sometimes referred to as your "leave."

*Notational Gameboard Design © 1975 Selchow & Righter Company, printed with
permission.

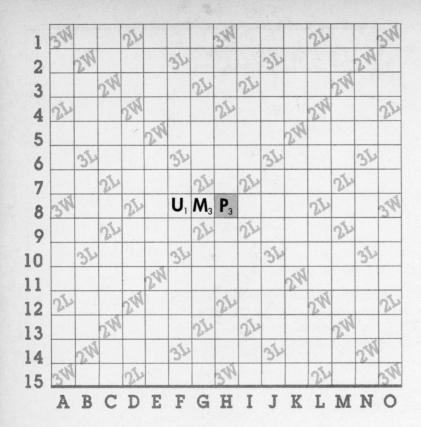

DIAGRAM 27

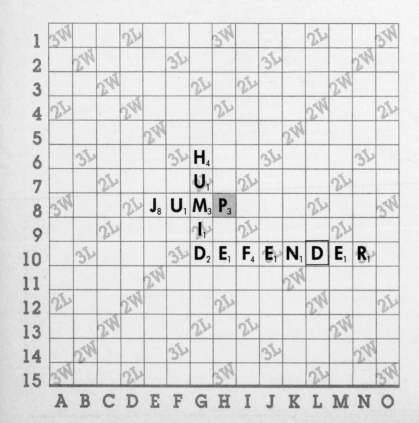

DIAGRAM 28

DEFINITIONS

Bingo (bonus play, seven bagger)	Any play using all seven letters and earning the 50-point bonus. These three terms are interchangeable.
DLS	Double letter score
Double-cross	Using a letter in two directions at once
Dumping	Playing a word solely to get rid of inflexible letters
Duplication	Two or more of the same letter
DWS	Double word score
Fishing	Replacing one or more letters in search of a bingo or for a valuable tile
Good letters	Letters that combine well with other letters in your rack. A letter can be good or bad depending on what other letters you have. The Q with no U is bad. The Q with a U can be very good.
Hot spots	Good high-scoring spaces open and ready to be played on
Inflexible tiles	Letters that don't combine well with the other letters in your rack, or with the letters on the board
Leave	The letters you keep in your rack when you make a play
Mice	Two or more S tiles
Mighty Mouse	An S
OSPD	*Official Scrabble® Players' Dictionary*
Premium Square	A colored square on the board that gives scoring instructions. Note that this includes the center star.

Passing (or exchanging)	Giving up your turn to replace one to seven letters
Rack balance	Ratio of consonants to vowels. Or how well the letters in your rack work together to make words
TLS	Triple letter score
TWS	Triple word score

SECTION

ONE

INTRODUCTION

In the first section of this book, the objective will be to introduce good habits and general guidelines. As in any endeavor, good basics are essential, so we'll look at them in depth.

If you're like most readers, you've peeked ahead to see what this book offers. You may even be feeling a bit apprehensive at some of the chapter headings, i.e., "Rack Balance," "Q Strategies," and "Dumping." If so, don't. All of these concepts are easy to understand. Actually, of all the games I have ever played, it is easier to play competitive Scrabble® than just about any other game, and you can enjoy it immediately.

As with any other game, you can learn to play as well as you want to. Want to be a once-a-month player? No problem. Read the introduction. Want to be the family champ? Check section 2 (Advanced). Want to beat that English major who "never loses"? You'll find the answers in section 3 (Games).

One last observation before getting into specifics. The early emphasis in this book is *not* on finding the best play or the most esoteric word. That will come later. For now, the question is, "Given two or more plays, what makes one better than the other?"

A CHECKLIST FOR FINDING THE BEST PLAY

When you are deciding on your play, there is a general checklist you should refer to so that you will not overlook any opportunities. Some of the items in the checklist will be new to you. They are offered here so that you develop an early awareness of them. Learning what they mean will come later.

At this moment, you should not be concerned that you don't have much experience at finding words in a group of seven letters. Believe me, the knack will develop as you play the game. After a little while, you will be finding words you didn't realize you knew, and you will be finding lots of them.

Here is the set of guidelines for finding the best play:

1. Do you have a bingo? You won't find too many bingos until you gain experience. In the meantime, you should get into the habit of thinking about them.

2. Prefixes and suffixes: One of the first things you should look for in your rack are prefixes and suffixes. Many, many words include a prefix, a suffix, or both.

Keep an eye out for opportunities like these:

    Prefixes: BE, MIS, PRE, RE, OUT, UN
    Suffixes: ED, ER, EST, IER, IES, IEST, ING, ISM

3. Are there any "hot spots" on the board that offer good scoring potential? You'll usually look first for TWSs (triple word spaces), but there are many other good situations worth looking for. Often, you will find that your best play is dictated more by the board than by your rack.

4. Are any of your high-point consonants playable on a hot spot? Perhaps there is a double-cross available.

5. Do you have the Q? If so, you should think about getting rid of it. It's often best to play the Q, even if just for a few points. Just because it's worth 10 points doesn't mean it's a good thing to have. (See Q strategies, p. 163).

6. If none of the above seems feasible, try to find a play that prepares your rack for future turns. If you have some letters you don't want, try to get rid of them.

7. Rack balance: This is a general strategy that says you should plan ahead. Don't automatically play each turn for the most points available now. Remember that your final score is the sum of all your turns. Getting one big play now and two or three little plays later doesn't look good in the final tally. This concept pervades almost every aspect of Scrabble®.

RACK BALANCE

Rack balance is one of the easier Scrabble® concepts to understand, and certainly no concept is more important. Unfortunately, many Scrabble® players have never heard of it, and they continue to make the same mistakes over and over again.

This short introduction to rack balance is simply an effort to make you aware of it, which, in turn, will help you to appreciate its importance.

What is rack balance? Rack balance, or rack management, is simply an awareness that you can't play every turn as if it were your last. You have to play for the future as well as the present. If you play off all your good letters and keep dreck in your rack, you may score well on the present turn, but your future plays will be painful indeed. Not unlike killing the goose that laid the golden egg.

In general, what this means is that when you choose your play, you should try to select one that leaves you with flexible letters. If, after your play, your remaining letters are something like ERS, ADRT, IONT, AES, or even QU, you can reasonably hope that your new tiles will combine to give you a good play.

If, after your play, your remaining letters look like IIC, UGWY, OOOK, JTTV, or AAAO, you are in for bad times.

Note the qualities of good tiles as opposed to bad tiles:

1. Good tiles include a balance of both vowels and consonants.

2. Good tiles are flexible—i.e., they will combine with one another and with those on the board.

3. Good tiles seldom include duplicate letters. This has to be qualified somewhat because some letters sustain duplication quite nicely. EE, SS, and TT are not bad at all. As your experience grows, you will discover which pairs are good, which are poor, and which are bad. This will be covered in the next section.

On the other hand, there are a number of things that make tiles "bad":

1. All vowels or all consonants—AIOU or CJTW.

2. Tiles that are inflexible—ABIW includes both vowels and consonants, but they combine poorly.

3. Duplication: AT is a good two-letter combination, but it suffers when you have two of them—i.e., AATT.
   There are two reasons why duplication is bad. One reason is that it is harder to find a good play. The more duplication you have, the fewer words you can make. A second reason is that you may draw a third tile, giving you three of a kind. If you keep, say, two I tiles and draw a third, you will have problems.

4. Too many high-point tiles may present problems. If you draw, say, ACJZ, or CFUW, or HKMY, you won't get many bingos. High-point tiles can provide good scoring plays, but they may not. When you have three or four letters that don't "fit," your rack can feel constricted for two or three turns. For instance, these letters are hard to work with: QW, FV, VW, KM, just to name a few.
   In general, two 3-point or higher tiles are quite enough. Therefore, when possible, you should try not to have more than one remaining when you finish your turn.

Incidentally, if you get the impression that bingos are important, well, they are, but they are hardly common. Between 65 and 75 percent of your plays will be of three to five letters. Some will be of two or six letters. These nonbingo plays will account for over 90 percent of your score until you become proficient. Even the best players score most of their points from shorter intermediate plays.

Is there such a thing as a bad tile? No. No tile, in itself, is bad. A tile becomes bad only when it is part of an inflexible rack.

Take an A. Do you like it? If your other letters are AAIOTT, you certainly don't like it. But if your other tiles are EINRST, you love it.

Take the Q. If any tile can be thought of as bad, it's the Q. But even the Q can be good. If you have a U also, you have the assurance that you can play the Q sooner or later.

Take the S. Next to the blank, the S is the second most valuable tile. But if your rack consists of AIRSSS, you can do without another S.

Remember, no tile is bad. Its value is always based on the other letters in your rack, plus the available letters on the board.

DIAGRAM 29

THE PRICE OF RACK BALANCE

The concept of rack balance is so important that a good player will often sacrifice a few points on a play in order to keep a playable rack.

Two samples now, and lots more later.

In diagram 29, your opponent played TOWN at **8-E**. Your rack is AAIORSW (indicated in the lower left-hand corner of the diagram). Which of the following two plays would you choose?

Which play
is better?

    1. **AWAIT(ORS)**   at **E-4**   16 points; or
    2. **ROWS(AAI)**   at **I-5**   19 points

Even though play 2 scores more than play 1, play 1 is better because it keeps good letters. ORS is far more flexible than AAI. How would you feel if you kept AAI and drew another A or another I?

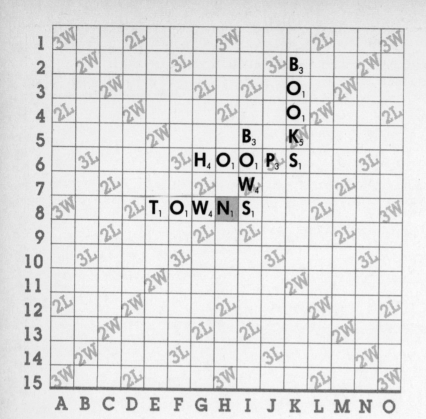

DIAGRAM 30

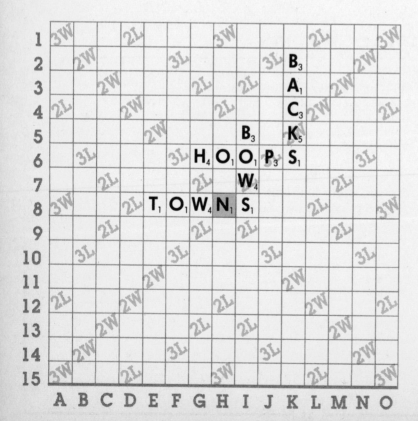

DIAGRAM 31

Essentially, with other things being equal, you are saying that ORS is worth 3 points more than AAI.

Diagrams 30 and 31 are much the same.

1. **BOOKS(AC)** at **K-2** 32 points; or
2. **BACKS(OO)** at **K-2** 36 points

Is BOOKS or BACKS the correct play?
(Compare diagrams 30 and 31.)

Again, you should pay 4 points in order to keep some reasonable letters. Play BOOKS(AC). Sacrifice.

There is a little exercise you can try if you aren't yet convinced about keeping good letters.

Take ERT from the tile bag. This is an excellent combination to hold.

Take VTU from the tile bag. This is not a particularly good combination to hold.

Now draw four random tiles from the bag and compare how well they match up with ERT and VTU. Try ten or so samples. Scary, isn't it?

Think of rack balance as an investment in the future. Losing a few points on the current play is a small price to pay for constant good potential on the next play. It's your total score that counts. One good-scoring play and three poor ones produce a poor average. Better to get four reasonable plays.

Rack balance obviously is not your only consideration when planning your play. The trouble is that it is frequently not considered at all. The important thing now is that you be aware of it. More later.

THE FIRST PLAY

In Scrabble®, as in every other game, someone has to make the first move. Admittedly, this is hardly a surprising observation. What is a surprise to many, however, is the consequence of the opening play.

Do you play bridge? If so, reflect on the importance of the opening lead. How many contracts were made because the defense made the wrong lead?

Do you play chess? How many books have been written on the opening move? Did you ever try P-KR3?

Or perhaps golf is your game. What happens when you tee off into the rough, or into a creek, or, worse, off your foot?

In all these games, your success or failure could be traced to your initial effort. And so it is with Scrabble®. A good, sound first play is instrumental in getting the game off to a good start.

What should you think about when you make the first play? Is rack balance important this early? Does it matter where you play your word? Should you go for the highest play possible?

Let's take these one at a time.

DOES RACK BALANCE MATTER WHEN YOU CHOOSE YOUR OPENING MOVE?

Yes. Very much so. From the first play to the last, you should consider rack balance. Good balance is instrumental in getting bingos, and in general makes for easier and better plays.

You start with AACIIRY in your rack. Should you play RACY(AII) for 18 points? or AIRY(ACI) for 14?

Play AIRY for 14. This costs 4 points but avoids keeping AII. Three vowels are bad, and having two I tiles makes it worse.

WHEN YOU GO FIRST, DOES IT MATTER WHERE YOU PLAY YOUR WORD?

Yes. For the moment, assume your word is a four-letter word, or less, so that your score is the same wherever you put it.

Let's say you have decided to start with the word FAME. Wherever you play it, you get 18 points. Just put it out there and collect your score? Not quite. There are four possible ways to play FAME, and two of them are bad, one horribly so.

To see how this works, look at diagram 32. FAME was played at **8-F**. This is a very dangerous placement because it leaves a vowel next to each of the four double letter scores (DLSs) surrounding the center star. This is dangerous because it lets your opponent make a play such as HAM at **7-G**. This adds up thus:

```
HAM  =  15
 HA  =   9
 AM  =   4
 ME  =   7, total 35 points
```

The reason FAME at **8-F** worked so poorly is that it allowed your opponent to play two high-scoring consonants on DLSs. Then, to make matters worse, these consonants scored in two directions at once. In this case the H and the M in HAM scored four times their normal value. (When you play a letter so that it is part of two words, it is called *double-crossing*.)

It could be worse. What if player 2 can play the word WAX, as in diagram 33?

This would add up even faster.

```
WAX  =  25
 AW  =   9
 MA  =   4
 EX  =  17, total 55 points
```

Makes your 18-point start look rather pathetic!

DIAGRAM 32

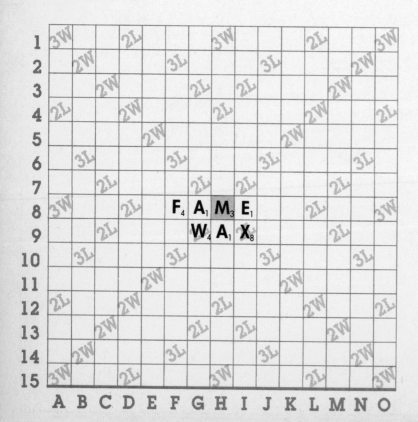

DIAGRAM 33

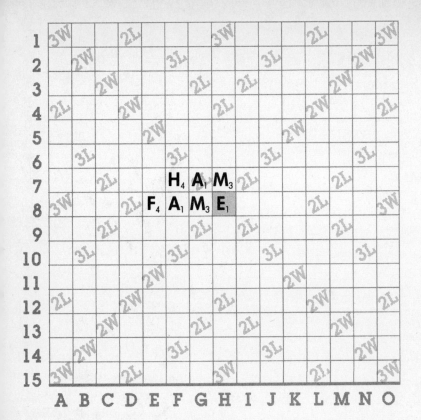

DIAGRAM 34

Was it wrong to play FAME? No. Your opponent had good tiles and was entitled to a good score. What he wasn't entitled to was a great score. What happened was that you played FAME in a poor location that exposed four double letter scores. It's true your opponent can't use all four of them. But he is quite likely to use two of them, and that can be expensive.

Rule—Try to avoid placing vowels next to the DLSs on your opening turn. We will expand on this rule later.

Look what happens if you play FAME at **8-E** (diagram 34). This placement of FAME doesn't leave a vowel next to a DLS; in other words, it doesn't "expose" a DLS. Player 2 can plan HAM or WAX, as before, but the totals would be HAM for 23, instead of 35.

$$HAM = 9$$
$$HA = 5$$
$$AM = 5$$
$$ME = 4, \text{ total 23 points}$$

And WAX would be worth 33 instead of 55. These would still be good plays, but hardly worth the farm. Note that if your opponent is going

DIAGRAM 35

to have good letters, he is going to have good plays. This you can't control, but you can keep his good plays from being great plays by being careful. In this case, careful means not putting vowels next to those double letter scores (DLSs). Don't give away cheap points!

A good exercise for you would be to compare the remaining two starting positions for the word FAME. See if either is dangerous, and why.

The discussion of FAME looked at a placement that exposed no DLSs. Some of the time, your word will expose only two DLSs. In diagram 35, the word LEAP was played at **8-E**. This placement "exposes" only two DLSs. Your opponent may be able to double-cross a high-scoring consonant, but he won't be able to double-cross two of them. In diagram 35, your opponent played WAX, putting both the W and the X on a DLS. But because there is no double-cross, WAX is worth only 25 points.

When your opening word is five letters or longer, you have additional considerations:

DIAGRAM 36

1. According to where you play it, your score can be affected.

2. Also, according to where you play it, you may allow your opponent to add a prefix or a suffix and reach a triple word score (TWS).

Take the word BEACH. Should you start at **8-D**, **8-E**, **8-F**, **8-G**, or **8-H**?

If you start at **8-D**, as in diagram 36, the 3-point B tile falls on the DLS at **8-D**. This play is worth 30 points. If you start at **8-E**, **8-F**, or **8-G**, you will get 24 points. If you start at **8-H**, as in diagram 37, the 4-point H tile will fall on the DLS at **8-L**, making the play worth 32 points.

Should you take the maximum points, or are there other considerations?

In general, you should take the points unless there are mitigating factors.

Here are two reasons *not* to take 32 points:

1. If you play BEACH at **8-H**, diagram 37, you leave the E next to the DLSs at **7-I** and **9-I**.

Diagram with letters B₃ E₁ A₁ C₃ H₄ spelling BEACH across row 8.

DIAGRAM 37

2. BEACH at **8-H** leaves your opponent the opportunity to reach the TWS at **8-O**. BEACHING would be worth 48 points and BEACHBOY would be worth 60.

Best is to take the 30-point play starting at **8-D**, as in diagram 36. You lose 2 points, but they are well spent for the extra safety. No vowels are left next to a DLS and there is no prefix to BEACH that reaches the TWS at **8-A**.

If the first word you play is LAMER, it will make only a 2-point difference to you in where you play it. You can put the L or the R on a double letter score (DLS).

Let's say you start at **8-D**, diagram 38, giving you 16 points. If you do this, you expose the double letter scores at **7-G** and **9-G**. For such a small return to you of 2 extra points, it is not worth exposing a premium scoring space by placing a vowel next to it. It would be better to start at **8-E**, diagram 39, which scores only 14, but exposes no double letter scores (DLS).

Here I would like to offer a guideline that will be expanded on later:

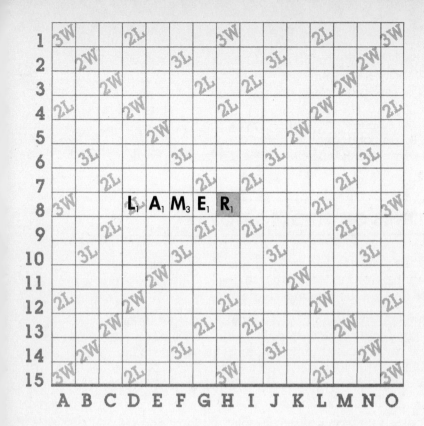

DIAGRAM 38

DIAGRAM 39

Rule: When your opening play *can* be placed on the board so as to avoid exposing a DLS, then you must gain at least 6 points over your next best play if your placement *does* expose a DLS.

If you choose to play LAMER, it should be played safely. The 2-point gain by starting at **8-D** is not enough to justify exposing the DLSs at **7-G** and **9-G**. Further aspects of this rule will be discussed in section 2.

TWO GUIDELINES ON FINDING WORDS

It's one thing to discuss where to play a word when you find it. It's another thing to find the word in the first place. I would like to offer a couple of hints here that will be expanded later.

1. When you are having trouble finding a word, shuffle your letters on your rack. If you have no success, do it again, and if necessary, again. You'll be surprised how many hidden gems you can find in a crummy-looking set of letters. Maybe you can find COCOA in AACCOOR, or BANJO in ABCJNOQ, or even the bingo BANDANA in AAABDNN.

2. When you are looking for words, make a point of identifying which prefixes and suffixes you have. Look to see if they fit in with the rest of your rack. For example, the letters EGINRST include:

   Prefixes: RE, IN
   Suffixes: ER, IER, IES, IEST, ING

If you look for these endings, you may discover RESTING and STINGER.

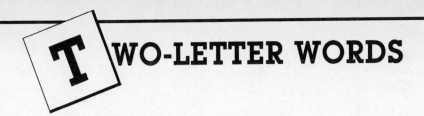

TWO-LETTER WORDS

One of the staples of good Scrabble® is a working
knowledge of the legal two-letter words. Regardless of whether you
are a crossword puzzle freak with an enormous vocabulary, or
whether you have a normal working vocabulary, you will often find
that a successful play will hinge on a two-letter word. Take diagram
40. It's your turn and you have BUTTERS for a nice bingo. The 50-point
bonus awaits if you can just find a spot to play your word. Too bad
BRASH doesn't take an S. Nope. Doesn't work. Does this mean you can't
play your bingo? No. It turns out you can play BUTTERS at **9-C**,
making:

```
BUTTERS  =  14
     RE  =  3
     ER  =  2
     AS  =  3, total 72 points, plus the 50 point bonus
```

Can you play
BUTTERS?

Nice. The trick here was to know that RE and ER are acceptable
two-letter words. Given that, it wasn't so hard to find a place for your
bingo.

If you intend to get at all serious about Scrabble®, you should learn the
two-letter words by heart. If you wish, you can find the complete list of
two-letter words in section two. For now, I give you this short list of "twos"
that you should know no matter what your goals in Scrabble®.

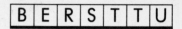

DIAGRAM 40

This list assumes you are using the *Official Scrabble® Players' Dictionary* (OSPD).

FA A musical note; the *only* two-letter word beginning with F

JO Lover; the *only* two-letter J word

KA Human spirit (Egyptian); the *only* two-letter K word

RE A musical note; the *only* two-letter word beginning with R

XI A Greek letter

XU A Vietnamese coin

Note that there are no two-letter words beginning or ending with C, Q, V, or Z.

STRATEGIES FOR SPECIAL LETTERS

If you have played any Scrabble® at all, you have experienced the ecstasy of drawing a well-timed S, and the agony of drawing an unplayable Q. And, accordingly, you said, or thought, something like:

"Beautiful."
"Where did all these I tiles come from?"
"Why did I draw that J now?"
"How can I ever get rid of this Q?"
"Where are all those E tiles when I need one?"
"Bingo!"

Remember? What you were experiencing was the basic fact of Scrabble®—that all letters are not created equal. Not at all. Allowing for normal exceptions, you will quickly discover that some letters are much nicer to have than others. Also, you will discover that certain letters require extra attention.

Which are the special letters?

The three most valuable tiles are the X, the four S tiles, and the two blanks.

The problem letter is the Q, which in turn lends special importance to the four U tiles.

Two other tiles that you have to respect for their value are the Z and the J. To a much lesser degree, the K falls into this group.

How should these letters be handled?

THE X

The X is an exceptional tile. Of the four high-point letters—the X, J, Q, and Z—it stands in a class by itself.

What makes it so valuable compared to the higher-valued Z?

It's worth 8 points, of course, but its real strength is that it is so easy to play. No other tile offers its flexibility and its potential for instant points.

There are five two-letter words that use the X. Curiously, it makes a two-letter word with each vowel.

By comparison, there is one two-letter J word, one two-letter K word, and no two-letter Q or Z words.

These are the two-letter X words:

AX An axe   **XI** A Greek letter

EX The letter X   **XU** A Vietnamese coin;

OX An animal   XU is also the plural form

Knowing these words can add a lot of points to your score. The X is so potent offensively that you can sometimes score 50 points by playing the X and no other letters.

Look at diagram 41. By playing OX at **D-3**, you make the words

```
OR  =   2
OX  =  18
 XI  =  18, total 38 points
```

By playing TAX and D at **M-2**, you make the word TAXED for 26 points.

By playing the X at **F-7**, you get

```
AX  =  9
 XI  =  9, total 18 points
```

The XI played at **13-I** is also worth a bunch:

```
XI  =  17
AX  =  17
LI  =   2, total 36 points
```

DIAGRAM 41

But the next two are killers. By putting the X at **J-6**, you get it tripled in two directions, giving you

EX = 25
AX = 25, total 50 points for playing a single letter

And, the last one, playing XI at **F-10** gives you a similar score

XU = 25
XI = 25
IT = 2, total 52 points. (Almost as good as finding a bingo!)

Notice the huge return you can get when you play the X so as to make words in two directions. X at **F-7** was worth 18 points, while the word TAXES at **M-2** was worth only 26, in spite of being on a double word score (DWS). The key is getting that X to work in both directions at once. In some circles, this is called a "double-cross."

Since there are so many two-letter words using an X, it is ideally suited to double-crossing.

Of the other big-value letters, only the J can double-cross. But because JO is the only two-letter J word, the opportunities to double-cross will be much less common.

THE S

The S, also known as Mighty Mouse, has a scoring value of only 1 point. Its real value is quite something else.

The S is not a scoring tile. It is a tactical tile that lets you maximize the value of your other tiles and the ones already played.

Here are some of the constructive things you can do with an S:

1. You can pluralize a word already on the board while using the S to form a new word, thus getting the value of both words. This is called "hooking," and is especially important when you have a bingo in your rack that includes an S. Other than the blank, the S is the best hooking tile in the game.

2. Anytime you have six flexible letters plus an S, there is a good chance you can make a bingo by pluralizing a six-letter word. For example, ACEERST makes CREATES. This quality alone makes the S a powerful weapon.

3. It forms many high-frequency endings such as IES, IEST, and EST.

4. Don't overlook the two-letter word SH. It's unusual and it makes a good hook. (See diagram 46, for instance.)

There are a number of useful generalities regarding an S. If you have only one S, you should not use it unless it gains you 7 or more points over your next best play. This means you should not stick it on a word merely to gain an extra point or two. If adding an S lets you reach a double word or triple word space, then you can use an S if by doing so you gain an additional 7 points.

Note that if you have two S tiles, you can accept fewer points, say 5, when you play one.

If you can make a word using an S, such as MASH, TRASH, or QUASH, see if using the S is gaining you the 7 points you require.

Take MASH for instance. You could also make HAM, and keep the S. CRASH also makes ARCH and leaves you the S.

QUASH might better be played by using QUA and retaining the S and H. Of course, if QUASH reaches a useful bonus space that QUA does not, then by all means use QUASH.

Note that I used the term "good letters" when describing the various ways you can use an S. Good letters in this context does not automatically refer to high-value letters. It refers to letters that combine well and are playable or nearly playable. For instance, the letters ADEGIRT may or may not be playable all at once, but they certainly can be played quickly. For example, you have plays such as: GRADE(IT); TRADE(GI); AIRED(GT); and TIRADE(G).

Conversely, BCQUUWZ adds up to a lot of points, but you won't be able to play many of them until you draw some letters to mesh with the ones you have. BCQUUWZ, in spite of their relatively high value, don't combine well with one another. You might get a good play by using letters on the board. But in general, these letters make for a poor rack.

Note: Good letters are letters that can be played easily whether they are 5-point letters or all 1-point letters. If your rack is BCQUUWZ, these 32 points worth of tiles will be of no value if you can't play them.

Much better to have ACEILNT. This 9-point rack is flexible and offers a variety of plays, including: CLIENT(A); ANTIC(EL); ENTAIL(C); and LANCE(IT).

THE BLANK

The blank tile is a contradiction in terms. It is both worthless and, at the same time, the most valuable tile in the game. Like the S, it is a tactical tile that, if used to advantage, will let you get excellent mileage from your other tiles.

The flexibility of the blank gives it enormous value. When you draw one, you should save it for a bingo or for an exceptionally good scoring play.

Expectations from the blank vary as the game progresses. Its greatest strength is that it helps you get seven- or eight-letter bingos. Obviously, you are more likely to get bingos at the start of the game before the board becomes too crowded. Therefore, you would prefer to draw it early, when its value is highest. Would that you should always be so lucky.

If you end up with the blank at a later stage, you should try to use it to maximize the value of your high-point tiles.

What your expectations for the blank ought to be depends on how much Scrabble® you have played. If you are just beginning to play, your main goals will be to improve your skills and to beat your opponent, preferably at the same time.

I suggest you adopt this approximate guideline. After you have played two or three games, figure out your average points per turn. Then, when you draw a blank, hold on to it until you find a play that meets these two requirements:

1. It will score more than two times your average turn.

2. The blank is contributing at least the equivalent of your average turn.

Look at diagrams 42 and 43. Let's assume you are averaging 17 points per turn. Which play do you choose?

[S]TRAWS(F)	at **M-3**	37 points; or
SWAT([ ]FR)	at **M-8**	24 points

Play SWAT for 24 points. It's true that [S]TRAWS gives you more than twice your average, but playing the blank gained you only 13 of those points. Keep the blank for bigger moments.

This guideline should be used only until you feel comfortable looking for bingos. When this happens, your guideline should be to use the blank for bingos or for 50-point plays.

Only near the end of the game, when big plays become hard or impossible, should you take fewer points for your blanks.

LOOKING FOR BINGOS WHEN YOU HAVE A BLANK

If you are just setting out to learn Scrabble®, you may be a little uncomfortable looking for bingos. Having a blank has caused more than one person to have a blackout, and if you experience time pressure looking for a good play, well ... welcome to the club.

Incidentally, there is a common apprehension among new players that bingos don't really exist, that they are figments of someone's imagination.

Not so. Only if you believe they don't exist will that be true. Let me assure you that bingos do exist and can be found. You will have to get some experience in finding them, but you'll find it much easier as long as you think that you can do it. Believe me, you can.

Here's proof. The number next to each of the following letter groups indicates that there are at *least* that many common word bingos that can be made from that particular group of letters. There are almost as many obscure bingos. Try putting each set of tiles on a rack and see how many bingos you can find.

1. [ ]EIRSTT	11		**5.** [ ]ABEEST	4
2. [ ]CIKLUY	2		**6.** [ ]ADDEIN	7
3. [ ]AOORRT	4		**7.** [ ]AEIRST	23
4. [ ]GILOOT	2		**8.** [ ]CEORSU	9

DIAGRAM 42

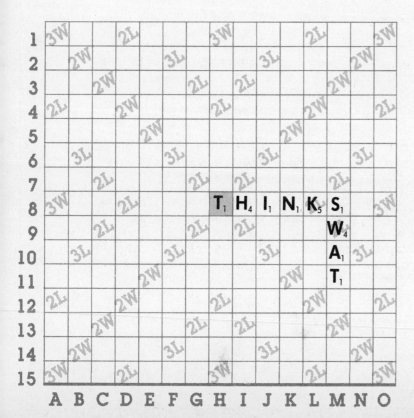

DIAGRAM 43

ANSWERS

1. □EIRSTT   [B]ITTERS   [F]ITTERS   [H]ITTERS
   [J]ITTERS   [L]ITTERS   [S]ITTERS
   [T]ITTERS   T[A]STIER   T[E]STIER
   TI[N]TERS   TRITES[T]

2. □CIKLUY   [Q]UICKLY   LUCKI[L]Y

3. □AOORRT   O[U]TROAR   ORATOR[Y]   RO[T]ATOR   ORATOR[S]

4. □GILOOT   LOOTI[N]G   TOOLI[N]G

5. □ABEEST   BEATE[R]S   [R]EBATES   [D]EBATES
   BETA[K]ES

6. □ADDEIN   DANDIE[R]   DANDIE[S]   IN[V]ADED
   D[R]AINED   [U]NAIDED
   [B]ANDIED   [C]ANDIED

7. □AEIRST   [B]AITERS   RA[C]IEST   TIRA[D]ES
   [F]AIREST   [H]ASTIER   RETAI[L]S
   SA[L]TIER   REA[L]IST   RETAI[N]S
   [N]ASTIER   RETI[N]AS   STAI[N]ER
   [P]ARTIES   TRAI[P]SE   [P]ASTIER
   [P]IRATES   TA[R]RIES   SATIRE[S]
   [T]ASTIER   S[T]RIATE   AT[T]IRES
   [W]ARIEST   [W]AITERS

8. □CEORSU   O[B]SCURE   COURSE[S]   SCOUR[G]E
   C[A]ROUSE   [S]UCROSE   SCOURE[D]
   RE[F]OCUS   C[L]OSURE

Looking over the above list of bingos, a few observations seem worth making:

1. Bingos do exist. Sometimes more than you imagine. But you have to look for them. Some people worry about not knowing enough words. It's true that Scrabble® rewards a big vocabulary, but it rewards being observant even more. Knowing lots of words doesn't help if you can't find them.

2. Even dull letters can have a silver lining. The second rack, □CIKLUY, doesn't look too promising, but it does have two common bingos (LUCKILY and QUICKLY), plus an obscure one, MUCKILY.

3. Often a set of letters will provide more than one bingo. When you find one, you should not automatically stop looking. Some people find a bingo but when they can't find a place to play it they get discouraged. Rather than spending another few minutes confirming that you really can't play it, or possibly lamenting for the sake of your ego, look for another bingo. Very possibly you will find a bingo that you *can* play.

Note that in each of the above examples, you had a blank that gave you far more potential for bingos than if you didn't have a blank.

Nonetheless, you should always look twice, blank or not.

T HE DIFFICULT LETTERS

T HE Q

Of all the letters in the alphabet, the one that inspires the most dread is the Q. It isn't always bad to draw the Q, but when it is bad, it is bad with a vengeance. I've lost far too many games because of an unplayable Q. For my money, I would prefer not to draw it. There are many reasons why the Q can be bad.

1. It is often hard to play the Q. If you don't have the U and if you don't have one of the few Q words that doesn't need a U, your rack is carrying a heavy burden. Having a nonplayable Q means you are playing with a six-tile rack. It's a little like playing football with only ten men.

Here's a short table to show you what you lose when you have a dead tile:

Say you have three tiles, ABC. You can make three groups of two letters, AB, AC, and BC. These can be played in six ways, AB, BA, AC, CA, BC, and CB.

If you have six letters to play with, you can make fifteen two-letter groups that can be played in thirty ways. This is what happens when you have a dead Q.

If you have seven letters to play with, you can make twenty-one groups of two letters and you will have forty-two ways to play them. The extra tile gives you 40 percent more possibilities, i.e., forty-two instead of thirty.

If you take six letters and group them three at a time, you can get twenty groups, each of which can be played six ways for a total of 120 possible combinations.

Add a seventh tile and you have thirty-five groups of three, which translates to 210 possible sequences. This time, the extra letter gives you 75 percent more flexibility, i.e., 210 combinations instead of 120.

As you can see, a dead tile *does* affect your rack, and the news is not good.

2. It is hard to find bingos using the Q.

3. If you get caught at the end of the game with the Q, it will cost you 20 points. It's like giving your opponent one free turn.

Look in your dictionary. Not very many words starting with Q, are there? Quickly now, name ten additional words that include a Q somewhere other than as the first letter. Well? If you can name five, you are well above average.

It's not bad enough that there are few Q words. The real kicker is that (with a few exceptions) you have to have a U to go with the Q.

So what do you do when you get stuck with it?

The first thing you do is a little homework before you sit down to play.

Here are three short lists of Q words. These lists include only 5 percent of the Q words, but they will solve perhaps 95 percent of your Q problems.

Words starting with Q:

QUA In the capacity of; it cannot be pluralized

QUAD A quadrangle

QUAG A swamp

QUAI A wharf

QUAY A wharf

QUEY A young cow

QUID Old British coin

QUOD A prison

Note QUO is not a word if you use the OSPD as your reference. It is part of the expression "status quo."

Words that include a QU:

AQUA Water

PIQUE To make angry

TOQUE A woman's hat

Q words that do not require a U:

FAQIR Religious person

QAID A Muslim leader

QOPH A Hebrew letter

These are useful lists to remember. I don't think a new player should have to worry much about learning new words, but for the Q, I would make an exception. You should read these lists until these words become second nature.

WHAT YOU SHOULD DO IF YOU DRAW THE Q

In spite of the fact that the Q is worth 10 points, and even if you have a U, you should take the view that you want to get rid of it as quickly as possible. Don't feel you have to get a big score from it. The longer you have the Q, the less chance you have to get a bingo. It's entirely possible that you will pass the Q back and give up a turn. Hopefully, an improved rack will let you score enough to make up for a lost turn. (More on this in the section on Passing, see p. 46).

It's so important to get rid of the Q that you should consider doing so even if you have a higher-scoring play available.

In diagram 44, you have to play from AAEPQST. Two possible plays are:

Which play
is better?

   1. **QUA(AEPST)**   at **F-4**   14 points
   2. **PASTE(QA)**   at **M-9**   30 points

It looks as if it should be automatic to take the 30 points available from PASTE. But doing so leaves you with the Q and continued problems. Giving up 16 points in order to get rid of the Q is a good exchange. Any time you hold on to the Q, you run the risk that it will turn into a burden. Especially so when you can't be sure of playing it later.

It's important to see what you get for those 16 points. You get:

1. No more Q. The value of this can be appreciated when you remember the times you had problems with it.

2. You won't lose 20 points by being stuck with it at the end of the game.

3. You won't have to pass the Q and lose a turn.

4. You won't have a dead tile and therefore an inflexible rack.

5. Your new rack will be far more bingo-prone than if you still had the Q.

6. In diagram 44 we were willing to sacrifice 16 points to get rid of the Q. It's conceivable that you would sacrifice up to 20 points to achieve this.

Note that in diagram 44, you did not have a U to go with the Q. If you had AEPQSTU instead of AAEPQST, giving you a U instead of the second A, you could consider taking the 30-point play. This is because the U gives you some assurance that you will get to play off the Q in the near future. You had no U, however, so it was good play to get rid of the Q as soon as possible.

AAEPQST

DIAGRAM 44

Note also in diagram 44 that you weren't given the score. In a later section we'll look at how the score can influence your play, but for now, general strategy only.

THE U

The U isn't a bad tile, but because of its relationship with the Q, it can present problems.

Obviously, if you have the Q, the U will be a valuable tile to have. The main question is: What to do when you have a U and the Q is still missing?

What you should do depends very much on how many U tiles and how many blanks have been played. If you have the first U tile, you should go ahead and play it if it is your best-scoring play.

If you have the last U, you should hang on to it, even sacrificing points to do so. Remember that it will cost you 20 points if you draw the Q and can't play it.

There are some circumstances that would cause you to vary from these guidelines:

1. If you hold a blank, you can be quicker to get rid of a U.

2. If one or two blank tiles remain unplayed, you can hope to draw one.

3. If there are places on the board where the Q can be played, you don't need to hold on to a U.

THE Z

Compared to the Q, the Z is a relative bargain. It is easy to play because it starts words with every vowel. Curiously, there is only one word beginning with ZU, ZUCCHINI.

Unfortunately, the Z is not that big a deal, scoring-wise. There are some nice scoring Z words but there won't be many bingos. The vast majority of Z plays are three to five letters.

Also, because there are no two-letter Z words, you will have almost none of the powerful double-crossing plays that are so common with the X.

As far as strategy goes, there isn't too much. It's possible to hold the Z for a great play, *but*, in general, I would not do that. The Z can hurt the flexibility of your rack and certainly cuts down on your potential bingos. I would not purposely take a poor score to get rid of it, but I wouldn't expect a bonanza either.

What you should do is to learn some of the unusual Z words.

Here are a few that will prove useful:

Words starting with Z:

ZAX   A cutting tool. Remember this one. It allows you to add a Z to AX.

ZED   The letter Z

ZEE   The letter Z

ZITI   A pasta

ZOA   The plural of zoon

ZOO   A collection of animals.

ZOON The total produce of a fertilized egg (plural ZOA or ZOONS)

Words containing a Z:

ADZ	A cutting tool	**FIZ**	Fizzing sound
ADZE	Adz	**IZAR**	Muslim outer garment
AZO	Containing nitrogen	**NAZI**	A fascist
AZON	A bomb	**RITZ**	Pretentiousness
COZ	Cousin	**SIZY**	Thick and sticky
CZAR	A ruler	**TZAR**	A ruler
FEZ	A hat	**WIZ**	An especially adept person

Even though the Z doesn't offer many double-crossing opportunities, there are two combinations worth remembering:

AX + Z = ZAX
AD + Z = ADZ

For instance, in diagram 45, you can play ZINC for 57 points. A nice double-cross. JAPAN, incidentally, means to coat with a black lacquer.

ZAX = 29
IN = 2
ZINC = 26, total 57 points

THE J

Most of what applies to the Z applies to the J. The one notable difference is that the J can make a two-letter word. JO—a sweetheart or lover. Even this one word is significant because it permits you to use the J in two directions. This hooking ability can be valuable indeed and should not be overlooked. *Note*—the plural of JO is JOES.

A few unusual words starting with J:

JAG	To cut unevenly	**JINN**	A supernatural being
JEE	To turn right	**JOE**	A fellow
JEU	A game, the plural is JEUX	**JUN**	A Korean coin, no change in the plural
JEW	To bargain	**JUS**	Legal right, its plural is JURA
JIN	A supernatural being		

Some words containing a J:

AJEE	To one side	**RAJ**	A ruler
DJIN	A supernatural being	**RAJA**	Prince
HADJ	A pilgrimage	**SOJA**	A soybean
HAJ	A pilgrimage	**TAJ**	Muslim cap

DIAGRAM 45

THE K

The K is included as a special letter because it has a relatively high value. Even so, it is worth just 1 point more than an F, H, V, W, or Y, which are worth 4.

The K has one two-letter word, KA, a spiritual self. This is the only two-letter K word and should be remembered for its hooking value.

Useful words containing a K:

AUK A seabird

EKE To get with effort

OKA Turkish unit of weight

TSK An exclamation

UKE A ukulele

WOK A working utensil

YAK To chatter

YUK To laugh

Other words starting with K:

KAB	Hebrew unit of measure	**KEP**	To catch	**KOA**	Tree
KAE	A bird	**KEX**	Dry stalk	**KOP**	Hill
KAT	A shrub	**KHI**	Greek letter	**KOR**	Hebrew unit of measure
KEA	A parrot	**KIF**	Hemp	**KOS**	Indian land measure
KEF	Hemp	**KIP**	To sleep		
KEN	To know	**KIT**	To equip	**KUE**	Letter Q

So far, I have included a definition for the words offered for memorization. The reason for this is that knowing what a word means helps in three ways:

1. It may be easier to remember.

2. You will know what endings it takes. For instance, if your opponent plays KEXING, you will know it is a phony because KEX is not a verb.

3. You can impress your opponent.

Note: It is generally a mistake to hoard high point tiles in hopes of a big play. This is especially true for the J, K, Q, and Z. Usually it is best to play these off in short good scoring words and build for bingos with more flexible tiles.

Should You Bother Learning New Words?

It's not mandatory to learn these words to enjoy Scrabble®. But the more words you know, the greater your enjoyment will be. You will find that when you have a stubborn Q, or an obstinate Z, it will be worthwhile to have a few key words in your arsenal. Incidentally, if you play frequently, you have a choice: You can learn these words now, or you can learn them one at a time as your opponent plays them.

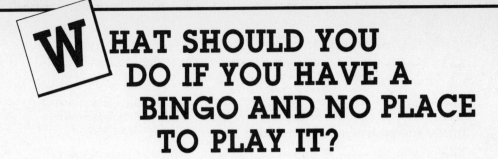

WHAT SHOULD YOU DO IF YOU HAVE A BINGO AND NO PLACE TO PLAY IT?

This is surely one of the saddest moments you can experience during a game. And equally sadly, you will experience it sooner and more often than you wish.

What you should do when this happens depends on a number of factors. First, though, two things you should *not* do:

1. Do not pass your turn hoping for a better board on your next turn. Your opponent, if he is wise, will know what you are doing and won't give you what you want. Instead, he will do one of three things:

   a. He will pass also and you will be right back where you started.
   b. He will replace some letters in an effort to improve his rack.
   c. He will play only if his play doesn't open up the board. Remember, he knows what your problem is, so he won't give you room to play.

   It's possible your opponent won't know what is going on when you pass your turn. But he will learn, as should you. If your opponent passes without drawing letters, you should do nothing to help him.

2. The second thing you should not do is to replace one or two letters in search of a different bingo. Even if you get another bingo, you may not have a place to play it. And you will have no points on the current turn.

What you should do depends on many factors: What is the score? How far along is the game? Is the board open or closed? How many points can you score if you play?

The enormous number of considerations makes it next to impossible to give exact instruction. Here, instead, are some general strategies:

Strategy 1. Play (do not replace) two or three letters. Try to play them so as to open up the board for a possible bingo. The score you get for this play doesn't have to be big. You are hoping to draw good letters and have a big play on the next turn. If you try this tactic, be sure you keep good flexible letters to draw to.

This strategy should be used when you are in trouble and need a big play to win. You shouldn't do this in general, because your opponent can also take advantage of the open board you just gave him.

Strategy 2. If you have a decent scoring play, take it. This strategy is the one you will use most often. A bingo play will get you in the neighborhood of 70 points, but you must consider your chances of getting one. Purposely minimizing your score while pursuing a bingo can be a fast way to lose a game. While you are scoring two or three small plays, your opponent will be scoring two or three reasonable plays. The net difference for him will add up quickly.

LOOK TWICE BEFORE YOU LEAP

A **common bad habit is that of making the first good** play you see.

This doesn't sound like such a bad thing to do, and often it isn't bad at all. But sometimes it is. The reason is simple: As good as your play may be, there may be a better one.

If you have found a good play after seconds of looking at the board—i.e., it just jumped out at you—the chances are good that there is something better. If you aren't under any time pressure, by all means, take another look.

If you looked long and hard before you found your play, the chances are you won't do better by further hunting.

This habit of taking a second look is just one of the many small things you can do to improve your score. There is no need to play impulsively unless you are truly out of time.

Look at diagram 46. What is your play with EEIQSTU?

There are a number of possibilities here:

What should
you play?

1.	QUA(EEIST)	at K-10	24 points
2.	QUIE*T*(EST)	at 6-B	34 points
3.	QU*OT*E(EIS)	at 14-F	36 points
4.	QUITS(EE)	at 14-A	38 points
5.	QUI*TS*(EET)	at C-9	48 points
6.	QUI*TE*(EST)	at C-9	48 points
7.	QUE*YS*(EIT)	at M-9	54 points

Curiously, these plays tend to be found in approximately the order given. Note that plays 5 and 6 are worth the same, but that QUITE is

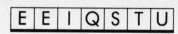

DIAGRAM 46

far superior to QUITS. QUITE lets you keep (EST), while QUITS leaves you with (EET).

How many of these did you find? Also, if you found QUEYS, did you stop looking?

It turns out that there is a much better play than QUEYS.

You can play QUIETEST at **L-8** for 78, which is an improvement of 24 points. And, if you look still further, you may find QUIETEST at **6-B** for 87 points.

If you didn't find either of the bingos, don't worry. But do learn from what happened:

1. Whichever play you found first, you looked to see if there was a better one.

2. You did not pay attention exclusively to the letters in your rack. Good play requires that you consider the letters on the board as well as the ones in your rack.

3. Even finding a bingo isn't reason enough to stop looking. There

C E E E H S W

Sometimes a
word can be
played in more
than one place.

DIAGRAM 47

may be a better bingo. Or, there may be a better spot to play the
one you have.

In a similar vein, what would you play in diagram 47?

The first thing you might notice is that you can add your S to AXEL,
which would be a worthwhile start. If you could add a vertical word
incorporating the S, you might come up with a very reasonable play.

Possible plays are EWES, SHE, SEW, and HEWS. One of these plays may
be best, but it can't hurt to look at all the options. Indeed, CHEWS(EE)
at **I-4** is worth 17 and AXELS is worth 12 for a total of 29 points. A good
effort.

But is it the best effort?

No. At least one better play exists. You can play CHEW(EES) at **7-D**,
which gives you a veritable plethora of scoring words.

```
    CHEW   =  16
  HAILED   =  10
      EX   =   9
      WE   =   9, total 44 points
```

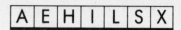

You have a nonbingo play worth 79 points.

DIAGRAM 48

You get 15 additional points for CHEW at **7-D** and you retain the S. An excellent improvement.

Again, the important thing was to continue looking. Having found, say, HEWS, you looked further and found CHEWS. Then, before playing it, you looked around the board to see if you had either a better word or a better place to play.

In some cases you will find a better word, in some cases a better place to play, and in some cases, both.

Diagram 48 shows another example of being flexible.

If you look only at your rack, you might find SHALE(IX). This plays conveniently at **K-8** and scores 28.

If you look elsewhere, you won't find another place to play SHALE, but you will find a couple of good places to play. There are many DWSs available, plus a DLS at **9-I**.

Some of these spaces offer play potential in both directions. Perhaps you can play the X somewhere. XI(AEHLS) can be played at **5-K** for 38 points and at **9-I** for 36 points.

Your rack also has words like AXE, AXES, AXEL, and AXELS. These can be played at **E-11**. AXEL(HIS) scores 42. A good score. But it leaves your opponent with a shot at the triple word score (TWS) if he has an S. You should probably just play AXE for 40. Or is there something even better?

Two additional hot spots worth looking at are the TLSs at **B-6** and **B-10**.

WHALES(IX) at **B-9** gets the 4-point H on a TLS and the entire word falls on a DWS. It's worth 40 points.

Can you do something similar at **B-2**? For instance, is there a five-letter word ending in H or X that will fit at **B-2**?

There is no playable five-letter word ending in H, but there is a five-letter word ending in X, HELIX. What's more, you can play it.

HELIX(AS) at **B-2** scores incredibly well.

```
HELIX  =  62
   HE  =  10
  ETA  =   3
  LAD  =   4, total 79 points
```

This is more than most bingos. Plus, as a bonus, you get to keep two excellent letters, (AS).

It all came from taking a second look.

WHEN THINGS LOOK HOPELESS

Many times, in spite of your care, you find yourself looking at hopeless letters with no immediate value and a questionable future.

There are many things that can make a rack of tiles bad:

    1. You can have too many vowels (AAAEIIM)

    2. You can have too many consonants (ABCNNTW)

    3. Too much duplication (AAMMTTU)

    4. Too many high-scoring tiles (FHIJKUZ)

Note that a rack is not bad just because it has only 1-point tiles. A rack

F H I J K U Z

These letters combined with this board do not score well.
(See diagram 50).

DIAGRAM 49

of 1-point tiles can be bad, but it can also provide you with high-scoring bingos. And a bingo is never bad.

Note also that a rack full of high-point tiles isn't automatically good. Too many high-point tiles tend to make for an awkward rack. And, if you can't play them, the condition may last for two or three turns.

Finally, note that when you rate the goodness or badness of a rack, you must remember to consider the letters on the board as well as the letters in your rack.

Look at diagram 49.

If you take the letters from example 4 (FHIJKUZ) and try to find a play in diagram 49, it will be an uneven struggle. Even with all those points in your rack, there is very little potential.

In comparison, the same letters allow quite decent plays in diagram 50.

QUICK(FHJZ)	at **D-8**	40 points
HAJ(FIKUZ)	at **7-G**	34 points
FIZ(HJKU)	at **12-H**	28 points

In contrast to diagram 49, these letters offer some nice plays.

DIAGRAM 50

Your choices in diagram 50 are:

1. A good score (40) and a bad rack: QUICK(FHJZ)

2. A decent score (34) and a poor rack: HAJ(FIKUZ)

3. A fair score (28) and a poor rack: FIZ(HJKU), but with some tactical gains

I would choose QUICK for 40 points. The 6 point gain over HAJ justifies the imbalanced leave, i.e., (FHJZ) instead of (FIKUZ). The *important* point of this example is that you didn't look solely to your rack. You have to keep in mind at all times both the letters in your rack *and* the letters on the board.

WHAT SHOULD YOU DO IF YOU GET A TRULY BAD RACK?

The first thing you should do is accept it. Bad racks do happen. Awkward, annoying, and irritating, to be sure. And, unavoidable. Like it or not, you will on occasion reach into the tile bag and draw out OOJKVVW.

When this happens, you have two choices:

1. You can *dump*, which means playing a few letters for a few points and hoping to get useful tiles in the draw.

2. You can *pass* any number of your tiles. You do this by drawing some new tiles and throwing away an equal number. But you lose the right to score points.

Which is better?

DUMPING AND PASSING

Bad tiles are not always totally without value. Sometimes you can salvage a modest play.

Look at diagram 51. This isn't the worst rack of all time, but other than the unplayable TITANIA it isn't very good, either.

Is this the time to dump or to pass? And, if so, what are the criteria?

DUMPING

Assuming you decide to play, as opposed to passing, your main objective should be to get rid of troublesome letters. In order, your thoughts should be:

1. Do I have a great high-scoring play? Then take it.

A A I I N T T

Should you pass seven letters? If not, what should you play?

DIAGRAM 51

2. If you don't have a great play, is it at least possible to get rid of bad tiles? If yes, consider doing it.

3. If your only play scores poorly, and if it leaves you with poor tiles also, then consider passing.

In diagram 51, there isn't a great scoring play, so your goal should be to play an A, an I, and a T. One possibility would be to play TRAIN at **E-7**, but it scores only 10 points and opens the board for your opponent.

This thinking, however, is in the right direction. A decent dump play does exist. TAIL at **7-F** is worth 12 points (TA, AN, IT, TAIL). And it uses the three duplicated letters. Further, it does not give your opponent additional chances because it doesn't open up the board.

The 12 points you get for this play are typical of dumping plays. You get a little something and you end up with tolerable letters to which to draw.

AINT is not all bad. AINT are flexible letters that work well with one another. Unless your draw is terrible, you should have a decent play

73

on your next turn, and if you draw well, you could catch a bingo. For instance,

PAINTER
WANTING
GRANITE
ANTIQUE   AINT is the basis for all
RETAINS   of these bingos.
TINWARE
NATTIER

Now consider the alternative of passing. It would get you no points at all, and your new tiles come with no guarantees. If you pass and draw another poor assortment, you are effectively giving your opponent an extra turn at no gain to yourself.

My guideline is that if I can keep reasonable tiles and get at least 50 percent of my average score, I prefer dumping to passing.

The circumstances of the game may give me reason to vary from this, but in general, it is a useful rule to follow.

Basically, I just hate to give up my turn. If I can find a way to use three or four letters and not give away too much, I'll do it.

Incidentally, once you have decided that you don't have a good play, it's much easier to find a palatable play. You just have to get it in your mind that you are looking for an acceptable dumping play and not a big scoring play.

If you can't find a satisfactory play, then pass, but do it only when there is truly nothing else.

HELPFUL HINT:

When you have some bad letters, an excellent habit is to isolate them on one side of your rack. Shuffle them around and see if you can visualize a word that uses some or all of them.

For example, in diagram 52 you have CEHMPRR. If you can't find a good play, you may want to emphasize getting rid of the CHMP group.

By trying various combinations, you may "see" such potential words as:

MUNCH	CLAP	CHIMP
PUNCH	MAP	CHAMP
PATCH	CAP	CHOMP
CLAM	CHAP	CHUMP

The last four words are especially good because they include all four

C E H M P R R

You have a 40-point play.

DIAGRAM 52

of the letters you wish to get rid of. If a suitable spot exists, you should consider it.

You can play CH*U*MP(ERR) at **10-C** for 20 points.

Can you do better?

Much, much better is CHAMP(ERR) at **F-6** for 40 points!

Most of the time, you won't be quite this successful. This technique of getting rid of certain letters is sound, however. Quite worth using.

PASSING

When you have a bad rack and are unable to find either a high-scoring play or a safe play that uses your bad letters, give thought to passing. In diagram 53, you have the same letters (AAIINTT) you had in diagram 51, but this time there is no good play.

Your best play is to pass all seven letters.

DIAGRAM 53

A A I I N T T

Should you pass seven letters? If not, what should you play?

Sometimes when passing you will wish to keep some letters and pass the rest. In the next section, we'll take a further look at dumping and passing, and which letters to keep, if any.

Fishing

Of the three techniques under discussion—dumping, passing, and fishing—the decision to fish is the most delicate.

The definition of fishing is that you pass or play one or two tiles while keeping five or six bingo-prone tiles. The theory is that, with luck, you will draw appropriate letters that will give you a bingo, or you will draw a premium tile that gives you a high-scoring play.

The problem with fishing is that if you have five or six good letters, you probably have a decent play available. If so, you will have to decide whether to fish in search of a great play.

Sometimes your rack is not so much "bad" as it is frustrating. Say you have AEJNRST. Lots of good letters here, but not quite a bingo. That J just doesn't fit into things. If it were an E, you would have NEAREST. If it were a C, you would have TRANCES. If it were an I, you would have RETAINS. The list seems endless. Anything would be better than that J. Actually, it is an overstatement to say that anything is better, but certainly many letters are better.

Should you throw away the J and fish for a better letter?

Possibly you should, but probably you should not. It depends on a variety of factors:

1. How many letters will help you? If only one or two letters give you a bingo, the odds would be way against trying.

2. Do you really need a bingo? If you are winning, or if the game is close, your best play is probably to take your turn. Only when you are trailing by a lot and truly need a bingo should you "fish." Fishing and succeeding may give you a big play, but if you are winning, why sacrifice points in search of an unnecessary and unguaranteed bingo? A win is more important than the size of the win.

3. Consider also if you can *play* a bingo, should you get one. What could be more aggravating than to fish for a good letter, to get it, and then have no place to play your word? Most of your fishing plays will come in the first half of a game when the board is still open and places for a bingo exist.

4. If you decide to get rid of the J, look first to see if you can play it. Is there a loose O on the board? You can make JO. Is there an OE or OUST or OY or UKE? Your J will fit in front of all these. Anytime you are thinking of fishing, look first to see if you can play the offending letters.

Remember that fishing works two ways—you can play or you can pass. Note also that if you fish a letter or two, you don't need to score as many points as when you are dumping.

I suggest that you don't fish too often. The trouble with it is that when you sacrifice points in search of a bingo, you can fall far behind if you fail to get the bingo.

Usually, if you have good letters, you will be able to score decently just by taking your best play and not worrying about the bingo.

Remember that three or four above-average plays can easily equal three bad plays plus a bingo, if you get it. Look at diagram 54. You trail 205 to 135 in a high-scoring game, and it's your turn with the rack we were just discussing—AEJNRST.

What should you do here? Is this the time to fish, or should you go ahead and look for a play?

You are 70 points behind.
What should you do?

DIAGRAM 54

Let's look at the conditions existing:

1. You are trailing by a bunch.

2. If you fish and succeed, there are decent places to play a bingo.

3. There are lots of tiles left. The game is hardly over.

Point 3 suggests that it is too early for heroics. Making a decent play would be a better tactic than fishing the J in hope of a bingo. Is there a decent play here?

With the rack you have, the J stands out like a sore thumb. It's very unlikely that keeping the J will give you bingo chances on the next turn. Therefore, you should get rid of it if possible.

With this goal foremost in your mind, you should look for a likely place to play the J.

Can you play it on **F-2** for a triple letter score (TLS)? No. Won't go there. Nor will it play at **6-B**, another potential TLS. You can play JET*S*(ANRS) at **8-L** for 19, but that doesn't seem like much, considering that you're 70 points behind.

There does remain one place on the board worth looking at. You can add an S to HALT at **E-8** and that gives you a shot at a horizontal word on the 12 row.

Possible words include JETS, JARS, or JEST. What you would really like to do is find a word that puts the J of the DLS at **12-A** and that reaches to the DWS at **12-D**. This double-double bonus would score enough points to compensate for leaving your opponent a chance at the TWSs.

It turns out that there are two such words available. JANES and JEANS are both acceptable words and are excellent plays. Whichever you choose, you will score 48 points, plus you are left with two nice consonants to draw to (RT). As a slight aside here, I would choose JANES for psychological reasons. My opponent may challenge it, which would be good news.

If you weren't sure JANES and JEANS were words, you might not have found this play. Not important. What is important is the thinking that led to making this decision. To fish or not to fish? To play or not to play? The thought processes are what count now. Doing the best you can comes later with more experience.

GUIDELINES ON FINDING THE BEST PLAY

Thus far, we've looked at many aspects of Scrabble® and what makes the game tick. We've looked at rack balance, we've looked at special rules for special tiles, we've considered reasons why the highest-scoring play may not always be the best play, and we've discussed reasons why you might pass and not make a play at all.

We've looked at various positions and compared play A with play B, play C with play D.

The one thing that has been missing is: *"Where did these plays come from?"* How were they found? What was the thinking in finding plays A, B, C, and D in the first place?

Obviously, the highest-scoring play is worth looking at, even if you choose to reject it.

How do you actually find the highest-scoring play? What routine should you follow?

Here are some guidelines:

1. *Do you have a bingo?* Bingos are explosive plays that can break open a close game or resurrect a losing game. You should give bingos your first attention.
   If you think a bingo is possible, and if there is a place to play it, then spend a little time looking for it.
   Some racks are more bingo-prone than others—AEHIRTS, ELNORTS, ADDEIRT, AGHINSW, and ADEERTW. These racks have flexible letter groups. They have balance, and there is little duplication of letters.
   Some racks look and feel distinctly "non-bingo-ish." ACCHIVW, AFIMNTU, BCDHIOW, FHJKOUX, and AEOIRSQ. The first four examples have poorly combining letters and the last has a Q but no U.

Much of finding bingos depends on your anagramming ability, and this will develop with experience. The important thing is that you do look for them. There is an old expression that you can't get from here to there until you take the first step. Likewise, you can't find your tenth bingo until you have found your first.

To show you the value of perseverance, I offer this small moment of embarrassment. When I was writing examples of "non-bingo-ish" racks. I included AIIMNTU. To my chagrin, it turned out that I had overlooked a seven-letter word.

Do you see it? It is, admittedly, an uncommon word. But a word nonetheless: MINUTIA (small details).

All this means is that you should not be too quick to give up looking for bingos.

How often you find a bingo will depend on your experience in looking for them. Bingos don't exactly grow on trees, even for experts. An expert usually gets one bingo per game, and may get two or more when the letters are good. But occasionally he won't get a bingo for two or three games in a row.

You should look for them because you will never get one if you don't look, but in general you should expect to play mostly three- to five-letter words.

Meanwhile, don't lose sight of the first basic of winning Scrabble®, i.e., rack balance. This good technique will help you immediately no matter what your experience.

Incidentally, if you feel you need practice looking for bingos, there is a bingo practice section on p. 174. Also, if you wish to review any other aspects of Scrabble®, there are quizzes at the end of this section and at the end of section two.

When looking for a bingo, do not restrict your search to the letters in your rack. Many times, your seven letters are tantalizingly close to a bingo. You must recall saying something like "If I had an M, I would have PREMIUMS." Maybe you don't have it, but maybe the board does.

Look at diagram 55. You have two racks with good letters, lacking just a little bit of flexibility. ACEGHNT feels like it needs another vowel. ABDEOPR feels like it needs another consonant.

If you fiddle around with the first group, you might notice the NG. An I would give you an ING ending and the group would give you TEACHING at **E-3.**

The second group, ABDEOPR, requires even more fiddling, but eventually you may discover PROBATED at **N-8.**

Note that in both cases, it took a prefix or a suffix to make a bingo. Not that a large percentage of words incorporate endings. Most don't. But you do need to maintain an awareness of them.

Having found a bingo, there are still problems. Let's say you have found a bingo and have a place to play it. Before doing so, you should ask yourself two more questions:

ACEGHNT

ABDEOPR

Each group of letters combines with a letter on the board to make a bingo.

DIAGRAM 55

A. Do I have additional bingos?

B. Do I have a better place to play it?

In diagram 56, you have ACEILST. These letters make up LACIEST. They also make up ELASTIC and LATICES. Look how much your score is affected by your choice of plays. Notice also how one play opens up the board for your opponent, while a different play does not.

Here's a list of possible positions and the score for each. You should note how the various placements affect the score and the position of the board.

LACIEST can be played at:

1. C-3	80 points
2. K-3	76 points
3. 4-C	79 points
4. 6-H	79 points

Board letters shown on grid:
- A-5: A
- A-6: P
- A-7: E
- A-8: T, B-8: R, C-8: A, D-8: I, E-8: N, F-8: E, G-8: R
- D-7: H, E-7: O, F-7: W
- D-9: H, E-9: E, F-9: E, G-9: D

Rack tiles:
ACEILST
LATICES
LACIEST
ELASTIC

Where can these bingos be played? (*Hint:* There are quite a few places. What is the highest-scoring play?)

DIAGRAM 56

LATICES can be played at:

1. **C-2**   78 points
2. **K-2**   76 points
3. **4-A**   77 points
4. **4-C**   77 points
5. **6-H**   75 points

ELASTIC can be played at:

1. **C-5**   69 points
2. **K-5**   94 points
3. **4-A**   75 points

Among things worth noting, LATICES at **4-A** and ELASTIC at **4-A** both open up the triple word score (TWS) at **A-1** and **A-8**. Also, there is a 25-point difference between the best-scoring and worst-scoring plays.

2. *When looking for bingos or shorter words, keep an eye out for those prefixes and suffixes.*

Common prefixes include: IN, EN, RE, OUT, MIS, OVER, UN, PRE, BE, and DE

Identify the
hot spots here.

Where would you
try to play?

DIAGRAM 5

Common suffixes include: ER, ERS, ED, IES, IEST, ING, ISM, IST, ION, TION, LY, and EST

When looking for a play, you should develop the habit of looking for these endings.

3. *If you have a high-scoring letter, you should look for a premium space on which to play it.* If you can double-cross it on a double letter or triple letter score, it's probably right. If you can play it on a triple word or double word score, that can score well too.

Often the best play can be found by looking for those hot spots on the board. They may dictate that you try to play in a certain area.

Rule: It is just as important to look at the board to see *where* you should play as it is to look at your rack to see *which letters* to play.

In diagram 57, there are a number of hot spots almost calling to you.

D-4. Perhaps you can put a high-scoring consonant here and get two doubled words. HOW at **D-2** is worth 28 points.

The triple word column at **H-1** is available. A long word using the A could be worthwhile. CASUAL would be worth 27 points. MAMBA would be worth 42 points. In truth, it is a bit difficult to use this triple word score, so perhaps it should be called a warm spot.

The triple letter score (TLS) at **10-J** is especially appealing. The X by itself is worth 50 points. An H, W, or Y is worth 26.

The triple word score (TWS) at **8-O** also looks inviting. Something like HOLD or WAND is worth 50 and WAXY would be worth 77!

The two double letter scores (DLS) at **7-G** and **9-G** would normally be worth noting, except that this time there are better plays available. The 11 row offers an excellent opportunity. If you can play a word from **11-E** to **11-K** using the N already on the board, you can score a *double-double*. Your word will be doubled twice, thus getting four times its value. STUNNED (**11-E**) would score 32 points; and SPRAINED (**11-D**) would score 44 points.

Note again the power of double-crossing a high-scoring letter on a premium space. A W at **10-J** for 26 is worth more than KNOWN at **12-I**. Even with KNOWN falling on a double word score (DWS), it scored only 24.

4. If you have no high-scoring letters, or if you can't play them, you should consider your medium-point letters—B, C, F, H, K, M, P, V, W, and Y. If you have one, you should check the board for double-crossing opportunities, or useful premium spaces, much as you would for higher-scoring letters.

5. If you have the Q, you should look for opportunities to get rid of it. Remember that it is often good policy to dump it for a smaller score than was available elsewhere. You might sacrifice as much as 20 points to play the Q. Hopefully, ensuing turns will be better for you. If so, you will regain the lost points with interest.

Repeat, do not hold on to the Q in search of a great play. If the Q sits in your rack for four or five turns, it will cost from 5 to 12 points per turn. How often can you play the Q for enough to make up for all those lost points?

6. When there is nothing dynamic to do, you usually fall back on what is described as your "basic play."

A "basic play" is one where your immediate goals are to achieve rack balance, develop the board, and/or advance the game. Your emphasis is not so much to score on this turn as it is to prepare your rack for future turns. You will play anywhere from two to five letters, and your score will be equal to or perhaps a little bit less than your average.

Good Scrabble® requires a lot of "basic plays"; perhaps as many as 70 to 90 percent of your plays will fall into this category. The idea behind this general approach is that by maintaining a balanced and flexible rack, you will be in contention for more bingos. While you may be losing a few points on a given play, you will often recover 10 to 20, or even 50, when your balanced rack allows you to find a good play.

The habit of developing rack balance will pay off in more ways than just finding bingos. Good rack balance will mean consistently good basic plays that comprise the majority of your score. Bingos are nice, but it is the "run of the mill" plays that do the work.

7. Finally, there is the question of making words. Given ACEFINK, how do you find KNIFE? Given ACEORTV, how do you find OVERACT?

   These things come with experience more than anything else. By using the guidelines above and getting practice through playing, you will improve much faster than you could have imagined.

Here are a few helpful hints:

1. Remember those prefixes and suffixes.

2. Move those letters around. Don't just stare at them and let your mind do all the work. Let your eyes help.

   For example, AEILOST has a bingo in it. It's a common word, but difficult to find. If you shuffle the letters around, you will look at various combinations. Maybe one will strike a familiar chord and you will find or "see" the word:

AEILOST	TALOIES	TAILSEO	SOIETAL	STALEOI
SOLATEI	LEASTIO	TOILSEA	SLATEIO	ISOTALE
LATEIOS				

   Looking at these letters in various groupings may help you see ISOLATE. If you are aware of and look for prefixes and suffixes, you may have noticed a few. If you saw ATE and ISO, you would have tried both and would have found ISOLATE.

3. Almost every newspaper has an anagram called *Jumble*. The idea is to untangle five or six letters to make a word. It's good practice and is worth doing.

4. If you have a few spare moments, take seven letters from the bag and practice looking for words. (Don't do this during a game.) In the meantime, just do the best you can and have a good time. That's the real goal.

QUIZ FOR SECTION ONE

1. What are mice?

2. What is rack balance?

3. Which are the 10-point tiles?

4. Which are the 4-point tiles?

5. What is a double-cross?

6. How many U tiles are there?

7. How many points is the K worth?

8. How many I tiles are there?

9. What is Mighty Mouse?

10. What is dumping?

11. What is passing?

12. How many letters can you pass?

13. What is a bingo?

14. Which tile is the best point-getter?

15. Which letters can't make two-letter words?

16. What is the only two-letter word beginning with J?

17. What two-letter words include X?

18. What is the only two-letter word beginning with R?

19. What is the only two-letter word beginning with K?

20. Can you think of another two-letter G word besides GO?

21. Name three words using Q that do not require a U.

22. Is ZAX a word?

23. Is JAG a word?

24. Is KAT a word?

25. Can you find a bingo in ADEPRSS?

26. What danger should you avoid when you play the opening word?

27. How many points should you get from each S?

28. How many points should you get when you use a □?

29. What is a DLS?

30. What is a DWS?

31. What is a hot spot?

32. What is a TLS?

33. What is a TWS?

34. Is QUO a word?

35. What is the OSPD?

36. What is fishing?

QUIZ ANSWERS

1. Mice are two or more S tiles.

2. Rack balance means you keep (or try to keep) a reasonable ratio of vowels to consonants. Also, you try to minimize double letters (two of one letter) as well as awkward combinations.

3. Q and Z are worth 10 points.

4. F, H, V, W, and Y are worth 4 points.

5. A double-cross is a letter played so as to score in two directions.

6. There are four U tiles.

7. The K is worth 5 points.

8. There are nine I tiles.

9. Mighty Mouse is an S.

10. Dumping is playing a low-scoring word in order to get rid of certain tiles.

11. Passing is replacing tiles in your rack with new tiles. You lose your turn when you pass.

12. You can pass any number.

13. A bingo is a seven-letter word.

14. The X.

15. C, Q, V, and Z do not make any two-letter words.

16. JO is the only two-letter word starting with J.

17. AX, EX, XI, OX, and XU.

18. RE is the only two-letter word starting with R.

19. KA is the only two-letter word starting with K.

20. GO is the only two-letter word starting with G.

21. QAID, FAQIR, QOPH, QINTAR, and QINDAR (Albanian money) are legal words that use the Q but not U.

22. ZAX is a cutting tool.

23. JAG means to cut unevenly.

24. KAT is a shrub.

25. ADEPRSS makes the word SPREADS.

26. When you make the opening play, try not to put vowels directly above or below the blue double letter score (DLS) spaces.

27. When you play an S, it should gain you at least 7 points.

28. When you use a blank, you should score at least twice your average score.

29. A DLS is a double letter score.

30. A DWS is a double word score.

31. A hot spot is a spot on the board that offers high-scoring potential.

32. A TLS is a triple letter score.

33. A TWS is a triple word score.

34. QUO is not acceptable in the OSPD.

35. OSPD is the *Official Scrabble® Players' Dictionary*.

36. Fishing is playing or passing one or two letters hoping to draw a bingo. You may score very few points on this play.

SECTION

(Advanced)

In the previous section, we introduced a variety of concepts and offered some hints on how to use them. This section will continue in a twofold fashion.

1. It will take a far closer look at some of the concepts previously covered.

2. It will introduce some competitive considerations and show how they can influence your decisions.

THE COMPLETE LIST OF TWO-LETTER WORDS (ALL 86 OF THEM!)

Here, as promised, is the complete list of two-letter words in the OSPD.

This list is the most important addition you can make to your vocabulary. It's nice to have a few Z words or J words in your vocabulary. They can make or break a game for you. But, in general, the little two-letter word is the glue that holds your game together. Note that the definitions are not always obvious. In some cases, the definition used is an obscure one (check the definition for "by"). This is done to show that a word can be other than what it appears to be. Also, it is very useful to know that a word takes an S. Wherever this is so, an S has been included. Note, for example, that "BYS" is okay.

AA(s)	Lava	**BA(s)**	Eternal soul (Egyptian)
AD(s)	Advertisement	**BE**	Verb
AE	One	**BI(s)**	Bisexual
AH	An interjection	**BO(s)**	A pal
AI(s)	Three-toed sloth	**BY(s)**	A "pass" in bridge and other card games
AM	Part of the verb *to be*		
AN	Indefinite article	**C**	(None)
AR(s)	The letter R		
AS	Adverb	**DA**	Preposition (of)
AT	Preposition	**DE(s)**	Preposition (of)
AW	Interjection	**DO(s)**	Verb
AX	Axe		
AY(s)	Aye	**EF(s)**	Letter F
		EH	Interjection

EL(s)	Letter L	OD(s)	Hypothetical power
EM(s)	Letter M	OE(s)	Wind
EN(s)	Letter N	OF	Preposition
ER(s)*	Interjection	OH(s)	To exclaim
ES	Letter S	OM(s)	A mantra
ET	Past tense of "to eat"	ON(s)	One side of a cricket wicket
EX	Letter X	OP(s)	An art style
FA(s)	Music tone	OR(s)	Gold color
		OS	Orifice, plural "ora"
GO	A verb	OW	Interjection
HA(s)	A sound of surprise	OX	An animal, plural OXEN, OXES
HE(s)	Male person		
HI(s)*	Interjection	OY	Interjection
HO	Interjection	PA(s)	Father
		PE(s)	Hebrew letter
ID(s)	Part of the ego	PI(s)	Greek letter
IF(s)	A possibility		
IN(s)	To harvest	Q	(None)
IS	Part of "to be"	RE(s)	Music tone
IT(s)*	Pronoun	SH	Interjection
JO	Lover	SI(s)	Music tone
KA(s)	Egyptian spiritual self	SO(s)	Music tone
LA(s)	Music tone	TA(s)	An expression
LI(s)	Chinese unit of distance	TI(s)	Music tone
LO	Interjection	TO	Preposition
MA(s)	Mother	UN(s)	Pronoun
ME	One's self	UP(s)	To raise
MI	A musical note	US	Pronoun
MU	A Greek letter	UT(s)	French music tone
MY	Of one's self	V	(None)
NA	No	WE	Pronoun
NO(s)	No	WO(s)	Use
NU(s)	Greek letter	XI(s)	Greek letter

XU	Vietnamese coin, plural XU	**YE(s)**[*]	Pronoun
YA	Pronoun	**Z**	(None)

[*]Adding an S to this two-letter word creates a new word, not a plural.

Here is a reverse list of words, ending in a given letter:

AA	OH	UP
BA	SH	
DA		Q (None)
FA	AI	AR
HA	BI	ER
KA	HI	OR
LA	LI	
MA	MI	AS
NA	PI	ES
PA	SI	IS
TA	TI	OS
YA	XI	US
B (None)	J (None)	AT
		ET
C (None)	K (None)	IT
		UT
	EL	
AD		MU
ID	AM	NU
OD	EM	XU
	OM	
AE		V (None)
BE	AN	
DE	EN	AW
HE	IN	OW
ME	ON	
OE	UN	AX
PE		EX
RE	BO	OX
WE	DO	
YE	GO	AY
	HO	BY
EF	JO	MY
IF	LO	OY
OF	NO	
	SO	Z (None)
G (None)	TO	
	WO	
AH		
EH	OP	

This reverse list of two-letter words provides a few odd facts:

1. No two-letter word ends in B, C, G, J, K, Q, V, or Z.

2. Any vowel plus an N or S makes a word.

3. EL is the only two-letter word ending in L.

RACK BALANCE

In the first section, we talked about rack balance in somewhat general terms, i.e., try to keep an even ratio of vowels to consonants. Play off bad letters when possible. Try to keep flexible letters in your rack.

This is good advice for sure, but it does require a deeper look. There are many factors worth considering.

1. *What is the proper ratio of vowels and consonants?*

In General:

Best   4 consonants and 3 vowels
Good   3 consonants and 4 vowels
Fair   5 consonants and 2 vowels
Poor   2 consonants and 5 vowels

Obviously, there are letter combinations that will make a mockery out of this list. The word FRIGHTS has a ratio of 6–1, which sounds bad. But it certainly looks good.

2. *What can you do to improve your rack?*

Science vs. Luck

Up to a point, there are things you can do. You must recognize, however, that there are limitations to your strategies:

a. If you have a very good scoring play available that leaves you with, say, VUU, you are probably right to take the points. While it's right to sacrifice some points for keeping a balanced rack, there must be limits.

b. Sometimes, you just draw bad letters. If you draw to AET, you don't need to draw AEIT. That would leave you with AAEEITT. You would be blameless, but you would still have a poor rack.

c. Even if fate forces you to keep bad letters, the luck of the draw may come to your rescue. If you keep VUU and draw ACMS, you will have performed a minor miracle. VACUUMS is a nice bingo to find and anyone lucky enough to make a bingo out of VUU will be lucky enough to find a place to play it!

What all of this means is simply that luck always plays a role in Scrabble®, just as it does in gin, Monopoly®, or baseball. It's the reason that, on a given day, anyone can beat anyone.

Nonetheless, good play will be rewarded often enough that you should not need to rely on luck. If you work at keeping a balanced rack, you will far more often have a good rack than does the person who plays random letters.

Be aware that even if you do practice rack balance, you won't always have the good racks you want. A realistic goal would be to have 25 percent good racks, 55 percent average racks, and 20 percent poor racks.

WHAT LETTERS SHOULD YOU KEEP?

When you are able to choose, you should try to keep letters that are flexible. Remember that "flexible" refers to how well a letter works both with the other letters in your rack, and with the letters on the board.

Sometimes you will play a six-letter word, thus keeping just one letter. Much of the time your decision will be dictated by the game conditions. But on occasion you will have a choice of six-letter words and consequently a choice of which letter to keep.

Your opening rack is ABDEILO. Should you play BOILED(A) or BAILED(O)? You should play BOILED(A) because the A is more useful than the O. Also, if you should draw a duplicate, you would much prefer AA to OO.

Your opening rack is ADEHMRS. Should you play HARMED(S) or SHAMED(R)? This decision is automatic. Play HARMED and keep the S. Never use the S needlessly.

Your opening rack is ADEHNTW. Should you play THAWED(N) or WANTED(H)? You score more, plus you save an excellent letter (N) by playing THAWED(N). Would you rather draw to the H?

There are many things to consider when deciding which letters to keep. Following are some of them.

THE VOWELS—A, E, I, O, AND U

A. This letter works well in general, one of its strengths is that it begins a lot of words. You can stand a second A, but not a third one.

E. Of the vowels, the E is clearly the best to have. It can be used at the start, middle, and end of a word. Furthermore, it can stand duplication and even triplication. There is no other letter that keeps as much of its value when you get three of them.

I. The I is so-so, as vowels go. Its strength frequently is in suffixes and perhaps prefixes. ISM, IES, IER, IEST, ING, DIS, MIS, etc. You do not want duplicated I tiles.

O. The O is not part of many endings, but it is adequate for making words. Like the I, it is not good when duplicated. When you have an O, look for OUT . . . and TION.

U. The U is a curious vowel because of its relationship to the Q. One strength it has is in the prefixes UN and OUT. Two U tiles are horrible. It's the worst possible case of vowel duplication.

There are ten possible pairs of vowels you can keep. AE is the best, one reason being that you can stand to have duplication if you draw an E or an A. EI and AI are both good, although another I would be painful.

IO, EU, EO, OU. These four combinations work adequately toward word formation. They all will suffer if the I, O, or U is duplicated.

AO, AU, IU. These are not particularly good for forming words, and, as usual, you do not want duplicates of I or U. You would rather have EE or AA than AO, AU, or IU.

This discussion has referred a lot to duplication. Remember the side note that discussed a dead Q? (See p. 55.) When you couldn't play the Q, you were playing with a short rack that cuts down your flexibility by as much as 85 percent. When you have duplication, the effect is similar. It may not be as emphatically bad as when you have a dead Q, but when you have, say, II or UU you are not playing with a full deck.

THE CONSONANTS

Consonants can be divided into several groups. There are offensive letters, defensive letters, and bingo letters. Naturally, just to confuse things,

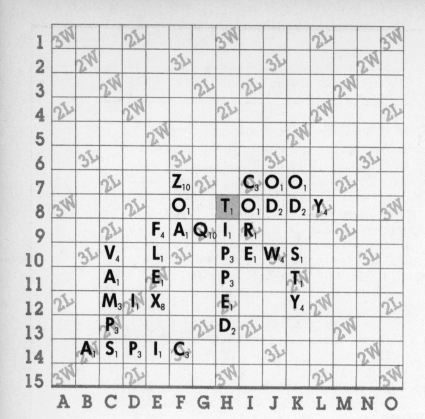

This is a difficult board to play on. If a bingo *can* be played, where must it go?

DIAGRAM 58

some letters fall into more than one category. Not to worry. The important things will be easy to identify.

DEFENSIVE LETTERS

C, Q, V, and **Z**. These letters do not make up any two-letter words. You can use them to cut down available bingo plays for your opponent, as well as to score points.

In diagram 58, it is going to be hard to find a bingo. The "B" column is blocked by the V. The "M" column is blocked by the Y. The 14 row is blocked by the ED ending in TIPPED, and the 15 row is blocked by the C. The 6 row offers a slight bingo chance if you can play along **6-G** and **6-O**. The rest of the 6 row is dead because of ZOA.

Of these four tiles, C, Q, V, and Z, the C is the easiest to use offensively. It combines a bit better than average, giving it useful scoring potential.

OFFENSIVE LETTERS

P, M, H, F, Y, W, and **B** are easily played and can be part of good scoring plays. Double-crossing them on DLSs or TLSs is an effective method of generating points. A general objection to them is that they are only fair for making bingos. When you draw any of these letters, you should tend to get rid of them quickly.

THE BIG ONES—J, Q, X, AND Z

The J, Q, X, and Z are offensive letters insofar as they score well. Usually, when you play them, your goal will be to score well, although on occasion you will play the Q solely to get rid of it. While the Q and the Z are good defensive letters, you won't often use them as such.

Even though you won't find many bingos using these letters, you should know that the X offers the most bingo words, followed by the Q, Z, K, and J.

Don't overlook the bingos that include these letters somewhere other than the first letter; for example:

X	Q	Z	K	J
ANXIETY	ANTIQUE	DENIZEN	AIRSICK	CONJURE
BAUXITE	OBLIQUE	ITEMIZE	MISTAKE	MAJESTY
BEESWAX	ACQUIRE	SIZABLE	TICKING	MISJOIN
PRETEXT	LIQUIDS	HORIZON	BRISKET	PERJURY
SIXTEEN	SEQUOIA	LAZIEST	POKIEST	SUBJECT

TWO-WAY LETTERS

B, G, J, and **K.** These letters can be used offensively or defensively. The K scores well and can be double-crossed using the word KA. The G can be used in an ING ending, giving it modest bingo potential. Defensively, there are no two-letter words ending in B, G, J, or K, and there are only a few two-letter words starting with B, G, J, or K. They are: BA, BE, BI, BO, BY, GO, JO, and KA.

Defensive Addendum

Remember: C, Q, V, and Z don't make up two-letter words at all. Additionally, no two-letter word ends in B, G, J, or K.

BINGO LETTERS

R, N, T, L, and D are letters that make words happen. They don't score well, but they give you flexibility to use your big letters and they help you find bingos.

Note that in addition to helping make up words, they also help make prefixes and suffixes. Only the L is weak in this regard.

Incidentally, the given order R, N, T, L, and D is the order of overall usefulness. The R starts words, it finishes words, it makes up words, and it is part of numerous endings: RE, OVER, ER, IER, for example. It is a great letter to have.

If you have ever watched the TV show *Wheel of Fortune*, you may have noticed that in the bonus round, the contestants almost always choose the letters LNRSTE. This is a wise choice because they have the highest likelihood of being used.

DUPLICATION OF CONSONANTS

Some consonants can stand duplication better than others. In general, the higher their value, the less you want them duplicated.

This is a relative statement, mind you. No duplicated consonant is truly bad. It's just that two of anything is not as good as just one.

One of the problems with duplication is that it cuts down on bingo opportunities.

As far as intermediate plays, though, there are many high-scoring dump words using duplicated consonants (see p. 103).

From best to worst:

Good:	SS, TT, NN, RR
Fair:	DD, LL, MM, PP, BB
Poor:	CC, WW, FF, VV, GG, HH

When you find yourself with a pair of "poorish" consonants, you should think about getting rid of the duplication.

Perhaps you have a good play using a word from the "Consonant Dump Words" list.

Perhaps you can find a play using just one of them, which at least breaks up the duplication.

Note that it's not quite as urgent to break up a pair of duplicated consonants as to break up a pair of duplicated vowels. This is because:

1. It's easier to get rid of duplicated consonants than duplicated vowels.

2. You are unlikely to get a triplicate. In the "poorish" column, there are three Gs and only two of everything else. Once you get BB, MM, WW, etc., you have a corner on the market.

If you have duplicated BB, CC, GG, MM, PP, VV, WW, or YY tiles, say, you should not rush to break them up if you have a decent play available. I would sacrifice up to 5 points to get rid of them, but no more.

CONSONANT DUMP WORDS

When you get stuck with a pair of duplicated consonants, you may want to play one or both immediately. Here are some dump words you can use to get rid of your duplicated consonants:

BB   BIB, BOB, BUB, BABA, BABE, BABY, BARB, BOOB, BULB

CC   CHIC, COCA, COCO

FF   AFF, EFF, OFF

GG   EGG, GAG, GIG, AGOG, GAGA, GAGE, GANG, GIGA, GLEG, GOGO, GRIG, GROG, HOGG, JAGG, MIGG, MUGG, NOGG, YEGG

HH   HAH, HUH, SHH, HATH, HETH

LL   ALL, ILL, BALL, BELL, BILL, BOLL, BULL, CALL, CELL, DELL, DOLL, DULL, FALL, FILL, FULL, GALL, GILL, HALL, HILL, JELL, KILL, LALL, LILT, LOLL, LULL, LULU, MALL, MELL, MILL, MOLL, PALL, PULL, SALL, TALL, TELL, TILL, TOLL, WALL, WELL, WILL, YELL, YILL

MM   MEM, MIM, MOM, MUM, MAIM, MALM, MAMA, MEMO, MIME, MOME, MOMI, MUMM, MUMP

PP   PAP, PIP, POP, PUP, PALP, PAPA, PEEP, PEPO, PIMP, PIPE, PIPY, PLOP, POMP, POOP, PREP, PROP, PULP, PUMP, PUPA

VV   VAV, VIVA, VIVE

(Since it's so hard to get rid of two V tiles at once, I'm including a list of odd words that end in V):

DEV, LEV, REV, TAV, SHIV, SPIV

WW   WAW, WOW, WAWL, WHEW

YY   YAY, EYRY, TYPY

THE BEST COMBINATIONS TO KEEP

From all of these comparisons, it is possible to come up with a few guidelines.

In terms of looking for bingos and for keeping a flexible rack, the best letters to draw to are RATES. Any combination of these letters (not duplicated) is outstanding. Whether you are keeping one, two, three, four, or five letters, you will have excellent chances for improvement. Obviously, the more of these letters you start with, the better your chance of success.

Even if you don't get a bingo, and the odds are you won't, you will probably have a good rack with which to work.

These letters are a pleasure to draw to: ER, ERS, ET, ES, ATE, ATS, TRS, AES, and AERS. Nothing is bad. The worst letters from the RATES group is the AE combination, and it isn't bad at all.

The next group you would like to draw from is ADEILNRST. This is RATES, plus DILN. This larger group is not quite as dynamic as was the RATES group. But it is excellent nonetheless.

A slight caution here: Not all combinations from ADEILNRST are good to draw to. You need some consonant-vowel balance in your letters when you keep three, four, or five letters. For example:

DLN: Good letters. Prefer a vowel, though.

DLNT: Good letters again, but having four consonants is bad. You would strongly prefer DELT.

DLNRT: More good letters, but if you don't draw some vowels, you will be looking at a very frustrating rack. Much, much better to have DEERT. The double EE, remember, is not bad at all. Even DAART is better than DLNRT.

AEEI: Good vowel combination, but with no consonant, you may be a turn or two away from good things.

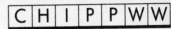

Your best play?

DIAGRAM 59

Much of the time you aren't blessed with RATES letters or ADEILNRST letters to draw to. When this happens, your considerations will be a bit broader. These questions will become pertinent:

1. Is it possible to hold on to a good combination? CH, PH, CK, and QU can be combinations worth holding.

2. Are there any combinations you should avoid keeping? For example:

ACKFSUW: Four defensive tiles

CFIOTUV: Three defensive tiles, plus poor vowels

CCIOSVU: Three defensive tiles, plus duplication, plus poor vowels

When these racks occur, you should make a very strong effort to rid your rack of intractability. You can do this by playing as many letters as possible with less emphasis on scoring. Or, you may pass six or seven letters. Don't carry a burden too long. It's sometimes better to give up a turn for a fresh rack.

3. Are there any letters that may be useful on an ensuing turn but that can't be used immediately?

In diagram 59, you have a choice of plays, most of them at **9-G**.

WO**P(CHIPW)**	at **9-G**	24 points
HOW**(CIPPW)**	at **9-G**	26 points
WOW**(CHIPP)**	at **9-G**	26 points
POW**(CHIPW)**	at **9-G**	22 points
WHIP(CPW)	at **B-5**	34 points
CHOW**(IPPW)**	at **G-6**	29 points

I would choose CHOW(IPPW) at **G-6**. It scores nicely, plus it gets rid of three big letters. Also, if you get lucky, you may be able to make a play at **B-2** on your next turn. Something like CRAW plus WASHY would be worth another 32 points.

WHIP at **B-5** would be worth 34 points, but it opens up the TWS at **8-A**.

The other plays score less than CHOW and they use only two letters. Getting rid of an extra letter from your bad rack is important. CHOW is a strong choice here.

YOUR CHANCE OF DRAWING A BINGO

If you are able to choose which letters to keep, you should try to keep the following combinations. The number alongside indicates the percentage chance you have of drawing a bingo when drawing from an intact bag.

Two-letter combinations with no blank:

RS — 24%	DS — 18%	SS — 17%
ES — 23%	RT — 17%	GN — 17%
ST — 22%	EL — 17%	IN — 17%
NS — 21%	ET — 17%	PS — 17%
LS — 21%	CS — 17%	MS — 17%
ER — 20%	OS — 17%	AR — 16%
IS — 19%	EN — 17%	NR — 16%
AS — 18%	DE — 17%	DR — 16%

Two-letter combinations with a blank:

□ □ — 80%	
S □ — 60%	
R □ — 54%	
E □ — 53%	
N □ — 52%	
T □ — 50%	
A □ — 48%	

If you like statistics, this list shows the number of times each letter shows up in the first group (two-letter combinations with no blank). Note the letters from the ADEILNRST series head the list:

S — 14%	A — 2%
R — 6%	I — 2%
E — 6%	C — 1%
N — 5%	O — 1%
T — 3%	G — 1%
D — 3%	P — 1%
L — 2%	M — 1%

Three-letter combinations with no blank:

Three-letter combinations— with one blank with two blanks

ERS — 33%	ARS — 26%	ALS — 24%	E S □ — 72%	S □ □ — 89%
EST — 32%	GIN — 26%	ORS — 24%	E R □ — 70%	E □ □ — 88%
ELS — 30%	IST — 25%	ESS — 24%	R S □ — 67%	A □ □ — 86%
ENS — 29%	NST — 25%	ILS — 24%	S T □ — 66%	R □ □ — 86%
RST — 28%	DER — 25%	NRS — 23%	A S □ — 66%	L □ □ — 85%
DES — 28%	IRS — 24%	EIS — 23%	L S □ — 66%	N □ □ — 85%
INS — 27%	AST — 24%	ANS — 23%	N S □ — 65%	I □ □ — 84%
ERT — 26%	LST — 24%	EPS — 23%	I S □ — 65%	T □ □ — 84%

The statistics from the three-letter groups with no blank:

S — 22%	A — 4%
E — 10%	L — 4%
R — 8%	D — 2%
T — 7%	O — 1%
N — 6%	G — 1%
I — 6%	P — 1%

Again, the ADEILNRST letters predominate.

B AD LETTERS TO HOLD

In addition to the duplicated consonants, there are a number of two-letter combinations that can sour an otherwise good rack.

Bad combinations are: WU, QW, JQ, JX, JZ, QZ, GQ, KX, FQ, FV, VW, BP, BV, PV, KM, KP, CM, UU, FP, FB, UV, and KV. Note that holding one of these combinations doesn't automatically mean that you have a bad rack, you may still have a high scoring play. The problem with having one of these pairings is that it makes your rack inflexible, limiting your choice of plays and hurting your chances for a bingo.

THE OPENING PLAY A SECOND LOOK

In the introductory section, we looked at opening plays and three pertinent considerations:

1. Rack balance—trying to keep useful letters when you had options

2. Not opening the DLSs for your opponent

3. Avoiding playing a word that can be extended to reach a TWS

ADDITIONAL CONSIDERATIONS

1. *Rack balance.* Actually, there's not much new to introduce at this point. Just remember that you have to start early.

2. *Opening DLSs.* When you make your opening play, you should try not to expose those DLSs. Remember: That means not leaving a vowel adjacent to a DLS square. Usually, you can avoid this by judicious placement of your word. (You'll recall we discussed this.)

But what do you do if playing safe costs you points?

In diagram 60, you start with AAAIMNR, which includes MARINA(A). If you choose to play it, you can do so at **8-D**, giving you 22 points, which is the highest score available.

Should you take the points? And if not, why not?

The reason you would consider not taking the maximum points here is that MARINA played at **8-D** opens up four DLSs, since that play left vowels (A and I) next to the DLSs surrounding the center star.

You can avoid opening up these spaces by the expedient of starting MARINA at **8-C**, diagram 61. This exposes no DLSs, but it does cost you 4 points since your M is no longer on the DLS at **8-D**.

A A A I M N R

Where should you play MARINA?

DIAGRAM 60

A A A I M N R

Is this a letter placement?

DIAGRAM 61

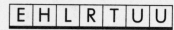

Where should you
play HURTLE?

DIAGRAM 62

Obviously, there are times when you will sacrifice points for certain tactical considerations. The question is, how many points?

Here is a rough guideline. Note there are two parts.

RULE: *If you CAN play your word so that you open up no DLS, then:*

1. In order to justify exposing four DLSs, you must score 12 more points than if you had exposed no DLSs.

2. In order to justify exposing just two DLSs, your score must be at least 6 points more than if you expose no DLSs.

If you play MARINA at **8-C** (diagram 61), you expose no DLSs. If you play at **8-D** (diagram 60), you expose four DLSs. But the gain to you is only 6 points. Better to play safe and lose 4 points.

If your rack is EHLRTUU, as in diagram 62, you could start with HURTLE(T) at **8-D** for 26 points. This would expose only two DLSs. You

E H L R T U U

Is this the correct place
to play HURTLE? Why?

DIAGRAM 63

can also play HURTLE(U) at **8-C** for 20 points, diagram 63, and not
expose any DLSs. Since you can gain 6 points by starting at **8-D**, you
should do so.

Some of the time your word can be played so as to expose no DLSs,
but it may require a dangerous placement. In diagram 64, you start
with CENOORS. If you choose to play CROON(ES), you can play at **8-H**,
which scores 16 and which exposes no DLSs. It does, however, expose
you to CROONERS or CROONING if your opponent can add an appropriate ending. And that is exactly what you don't want since it
would give your opponent a triple word score! Better to start at **8-D** for
20, as in diagram 65. This exposes a DLS for only 4 points' improvement. But it avoids the danger of a TWS.

C E N O O R S

Where should you play CROON?

DIAGRAM 64

C E N O O R S

Is it correct to take the highest-scoring location?

DIAGRAM 65

Does this expose two or four double-letter scores?

DIAGRAM 66

NOTE: Sometimes a play may appear to expose four DLSs, but in reality does not. In diagram 66, the opening play was BEHAVE at **8-D**. The V in BEHAVE makes no two-letter words, so your opponent won't be able to play through **7-G** and **7-I** or **9-G** and **9-I**. It isn't serious if your opponent plays through **F-7** and **F-9** or **H-7** and **H-9**. He will get two letters doubled, but he won't get them double-crossed. A big difference.

VALUE OF THE FIRST PLAY

Now that you have played a few games, it may have occurred to you that going first is good. Or is it? And if it is, how much is it worth?

The answer to this cannot be specific, but the consensus is that going first is worth about 10 points. You have the advantage of starting on a DWS, and if you can find a five-letter word you can use a DLS as well. Also, you get a look at five new tiles.

This DLS plus DWS offered on the first play is quite powerful for scoring purposes. If you can put a high-point letter on the DLS, you will get four times its value. You should try hard to take advantage of this. Only if your word opens up DLSs, or leaves a dangerous suffix or prefix for your opponent, should you be cautious.

A consideration we haven't looked at yet is one called "turnover." It refers to how fast you play your tiles. I should rephrase this: It refers to how many tiles you play at one time, i.e., does your average turn use two, three, four, or more letters?

Say you have DEELNOV and, all things being equal, you have to choose from EVE(DLNO) for 26 points or NOVEL(DE), also for 26 points.

The guiding precept is this:

On plays where all other considerations weigh the same, you should choose to play as many letters as possible.

The reason is that you are trying to put your hands on the blanks, the S tiles, and the high-scoring letters. It's like trying for a raffle prize. The more tickets you have, the more chances you have of winning. Since there are 100 tiles, each extra letter you draw increases your chances of getting a specific tile by 1 percent.

Likewise, the more letters you play, the more letters you draw, just like in the raffle. If you can look at 55 letters during a game, your opponent can look at the remaining 45. You will have 22 percent (10/45ths) more opportunity to draw the important tiles than your opponent.

You can translate this into points. If your choices are to play a three-letter word or a five-letter word, you should play the longer word if it doesn't cost you more than 3 points.

Roughly speaking, each extra tile you can play is worth 2 points in future potential.

This concept of turnover is important and should get consideration. It is not worth playing long words if it costs you rack balance or if it gives your opponent too much opportunity. But if there is no obvious cost or danger, then you should play for maximum turnover.

PREFIXES, SUFFIXES, AND HOOKS

Hooks

If you can add a letter to an already played word and make a new word, it is called "hooking."

Hooks can be in front or in back. Put an S in front of TANK and you have STANK. Put the S at the end of TANK and you have TANKS. The word RINK takes a B in front (BRINK), a D in front (DRINK), and an S in back (RINKS). All these single-letter additions are called "hooks."

There are hundreds of possibilities for lengthening words. You can use hooks, prefixes, suffixes, and sometimes you can add two or more letters that completely change the meaning of the original word. For instance, ATE + HED = HEATED, and MANLY + HU = HUMANLY.

Here is a short list to improve your awareness of endings and hooks. On the left is a word already on the board. On the right are some possible changes:

MARINA	MARINAS, MARINATE, MARINATES, MARINATED, MARINATING
HOOK	SHOOK, HOOKEY, HOOKY, HOOKA
LASH	CLASH, FLASH, PLASH
RASH	BRASH, CRASH, BRASHLY, THRASH, TRASH
TAMP	STAMP, STAMPED, STAMPEDE, STAMPEDING, STAMPEDED
COW	SCOW, LOCOWEED
FA	FAD, FAG, FAN, FAR, FAT, FAX, FAY, ALFALFA, BEFALL
XI	AXIS, EXIT, TAXIS, TOXIC, SEXIEST
JUST	JUSTICE, ADJUST, READJUST, JUSTIFY, READJUSTING
ADOPT	READOPT, PREADOPT
QUART	QUARTZ
READ	READD, BREADED, TREAD, THREAD, DREAD, BREADTH
VINY	VINYL

DIAGRAM 67

A E E L Q T U

Where should you play
EQUATE (L)?

DIAGRAM 68

C D H K M O O

C D H K O O S

What is your
best play with
each group?

These prefixes, suffixes, and hooks are important at all stages of the game beginning with the first play. You should be aware when you make a play if your word will give access to premium scoring spaces. Also, when your opponent plays, you should look to see if you can take advantage of it.

In diagram 67, there has already been one good hook. FLUX at **12-I** was added to HAZE for 45 points. There is an excellent hook available now for you using AEELQTU.

PUREE at **13-K** gives you the hook letting you play EQUATE(L) at **O-8** for 52 points. These hooks are sometimes obvious and sometimes not. It's easy to take LOVE and add an S, R, or D to it. It's less easy to realize you can add a C to LOVE, making CLOVE.

Sometimes hooks are hard to find simply because they are obscure words. But some common words are hard to find because your mind didn't make the right adjustment when you "pronounced" the new word. I'll bet when you added the C to LOVE, you pronounced it to rhyme with GLOVE. Right? Sometimes we are our own worst enemies. Nothing a little practice won't cure. The important thing is to have an open mind when you look for hooks.

What would you do in diagram 68 with CDHKMOO? KOS is a word (Indian land measure), which means you can put the K at **4-E**. This allows you to choose from:

COOK (DHM)	at **4-B**	27 points
HOOK (CDM)	at **4-B**	29 points
DOCK (HMO)	at **4-B**	29 points
HOCK (DMO)	at **4-B**	33 points
MOCK (DHO)	at **4-B**	31 points

Which play is right? Your answer depends on a combination of things: rack balance, points scored, and safety.

COOK is safe, but it scores the least number of points and it leaves a poor rack.

HOOK scores a little more, but leaves a worse rack. Also, it is very dangerous because it takes an S in front, making SHOOK. This could be very costly since it exposes two TWSs.

DOCK scores the same as HOOK, but it leaves a better rack and it doesn't take a front hook.

HOCK scores the most and leaves a fair rack. But it leaves a couple of front hooks. C and S make CHOCK and SHOCK.

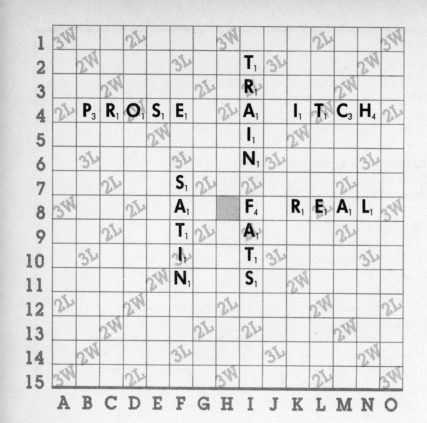

What hooks do these
words take?
How many points would
you score for BRAY at **O-1**?
How many points would
you score for YEARN at **O-4**?

DIAGRAM 69

MOCK scores adequately and leaves a decent rack, but it too has a hook. S adds on to make SMOCK.

The best play is DOCK, which sacrifices 4 points but doesn't leave a dangerous hook.

Curiously, if the circumstances were a bit different, you could make a different play.

Say, in diagram 68, your rack were CDHKOOS instead of CDHKMOO. Now, if you have been counting the ☐s and S tiles, you know you have the last S. You can play HOOK at **4-B**, and know your opponent can't possibly use the TWSs in the "A" column. But you can and you will.

This technique of setting up a hook is a very useful strategy. It works this way:

Say you have the word ITCHY, but that playing it would give your opponent access to a triple word space (TWS). It would be better to play ITCH and then on your next turn make ITCHY and use the TWS yourself.

In diagram 69, there are six examples of hooking:

PROSE at **4-B** takes a front hook U to make UPROSE.

TRAIN at **I-2** takes a front hook S to make STRAIN.

ITCH at **4-K** takes a back hook Y to make ITCHY.

FATS at **I-11** takes a back hook O to make FATSO.

REAL at **11-K** takes two back hooks:

   REAL + S   REALS
   REAL + M   REALM

SATIN at **F-10** takes three back hooks:

   SATIN + S   SATINS
   SATIN + G   SATING
   SATIN + Y   SATINY

Ideally, when you make one of these plays, you will have the last hooking letter. If you play ITCH, for example, you would prefer that both blanks and the other Y were gone so that your opponent couldn't possibly use the spot. If all goes well, you hope to add your Y to ITCH, and make a word reaching up to the TWS at **O-1** or down to the TWS at **O-8**. In diagram 69, a play like BRAY at **O-1** would be worth 56 points and a play like YEARN at **O-4** would be worth 53 points.

Note that the S that is the best back hook is also an excellent front hook. Don't overlook this when you are looking for an S hook.

Prefixes and Suffixes

There have been many references in this book to prefixes and suffixes. They are very important since many bingos and six-letter words include them. Following is a list of the most common prefixes and suffixes. Be aware of them. Remember trying to find the bingo ISOLATE The key was to isolate the prefix and the word fell into place.

PREFIXES

A—cross	EX—plode	OUT—side
AB—duct	FORE—cast	OVER—cook
AD—verb	HAND—book	PER—mit
AIR—craft	HEAD—rest	POST—script
ANTI—freeze	HYPO—dermic	PRE—view
BE—fall	IL—literate	PRO—ceed
BI—cycle	IM—bed	RE—tire
COM—fort	IN—filtrate	SEMI—dry
CON—done	INTER—act	SUB—marine
CO—operate	ISO—tope	TRI—cycle
DE—but	MID—way	UN—doing
DIA—meter	MIS—behave	UNDER—stand
DIS—play	MONO—tone	UNI—verse
EM—bitter	NON—stick	UP—lift
EN—danger	OB—serve	WITH—stand

SUFFIXES

like—ABLE	inert—IA	brain—LESS
mile—AGE	rad—IAL	out—LET
comic—AL	demon—IC	lady—LIKE
disturb—ANCE	log—ICAL	main—LINE
in—ANE	hast—IER	life—LONG
defend—ANT	phon—IES	poor—LY
milit—ARY	bead—IEST	door—MAN
king—DOM	hunt—ING	bar—MEN
heat—ED	react—ION	kind—NESS
train—EE	real—IZE	creat—OR
differ—ENT	full—ISH	vein—OUS
light—ER	real—ISM	over—TURE
green—EST	aerial—IST	in—WARD
con—FORM	odd—ITY	other—WISE
thought—FUL	anx—IOUS	hair—Y
man—HOOD	rest—IVE	

T HE FINER POINTS OF PASSING, DUMPING, AND FISHING

Remember these?

Passing (or, exchanging)—throwing away letters from a bad rack in search of a good one. Usually, you replace five, six, or seven letters.

Dumping—playing three or four letters hoping to fill in the good letters you are keeping. Usually, you are playing bad or duplicated letters.

Fishing—replacing one or two tiles in search of a bingo. You can do this by playing them or by passing them if they are unplayable.

PASSING

There are three aspects of passing.

1. You have to know when to do it. A common error is to pass more often than necessary. Remember, when you pass, you don't get any points. It's usually better to take a modest score than to take nothing at all. The times when it is right to pass are when your only play scores poorly and also leaves you with a bad rack. You don't want to make a low-scoring play and keep bad letters also. One or the other, but not both.

2. Curiously, some players take the opposite tack of never passing. Too often, too seldom, both are errors. On the average, you should pass a little less than one time per game.

3. The third aspect of passing is deciding what letters to keep.

Whatever letters you keep when passing must be excellent letters. After all, why would you keep average letters?

The trouble is that few letters are excellent by themselves. Most letters reach their maximum value when they are in combination with certain other letters.

KEEPING ONE LETTER WHEN PASSING

This is an easy one. If you keep one letter only, ranked in order of preference it should be:

1. The ☐
2. An S
3. The X
4. The Z

In the later stages of the game, you can pass the Z. If it is early in the game and the board is open, you should probably hang on to the Z. You don't want to pass the Z and have your opponent draw it while it's still easy to play.

KEEPING TWO LETTERS WHEN PASSING

Only a few pair of letters are worth keeping, and some of these come with reservations.

Always worth keeping:

☐ S
☐ X
☐ ☐

Usually worth keeping:

☐ Z

You would not keep this late in the game if you feel the Z will be hard to play.

Sometimes worth keeping:

SS—Optional. If both blanks and one S remain in the bag, you should only keep one S.

☐ E—Keep this when most of the E tiles are gone and/or when there are few or no open vowels on the board.

SR, ER, ET, EN, and ES—Keep these when both blanks are gone. The reason is that with both blanks gone, there are fewer good letters to draw. These letters become relatively good when the blanks are no longer available.

KEEPING THREE LETTERS WHEN PASSING

Always worth keeping:

☐☐ R
☐☐ S
☐☐ N
☐☐ X
☐☐ E*
☐ E N *
☐ E R *
☐ E S *
☐ E T *

Sometimes worth keeping:

ERN
ERS (Keep these combinations when both blanks are gone)
EST

IER (Keep this combination when both blanks and most of the I tiles are gone)

DO NOT KEEP WHEN PASSING

Here is a rough overview of passing:

1. If you can't score at least half of your average, consider passing.

2. If the board offers few good scoring opportunities, you can pass a little bit more freely, since your opponent won't be able to vault ahead.

3. If there are lots of premium letters left, you can pass a little bit more freely, since there is more to gain.

4. In the middle of the game, or later, I would consider passing the Q if two U tiles and a blank had already been played. The reason the middle of the game becomes important "Q-wise" is that the board is becoming cramped, making it harder to play the Q. Also, with 2 or more U's already played it's less likely that one will be drawn to go with your Q.

5. Most passing will occur before midgame, because a successful draw will be useful. What good would a bingo be to you if there were nowhere to play it? Since 60 to 70 percent of all bingos are played during the first half of the game, it makes sense to pass early.

Rule: When you pass, you must keep truly excellent letters. Something like AN is an okay combination. But it is not worth keeping when you can throw it away. Remember, the more letters you can draw, the better your chances of getting a blank, an S, an X, or a Z.

Note: If there are lots of E tiles left or if there are open E tiles on the board, you might decide not to keep the E.

ING—this is overrated. It is not flexible enough to keep. If you fail to catch an ING word, these letters won't help much toward making a non-ING word.

The reason you keep ERS, for example, is that these are excellent letters for making words. They happen to make a common ending also, but that's just a bonus. By comparison, the ING is great for a suffix, but not so hot for anything else. ERS is good for the construction of words in general.

IN, NG, ED, ION, IED—usually not worth keeping. You want to keep letters that are universally flexible, i.e., letters that will be useful for making words as well as for various endings.

By comparison, if you play a five-letter word and can keep AN, you should be quite pleased. AN is better than average. Compare how you would feel if you had WI instead.

Remember, when you *play* you have less control over the quality of the letters you keep than when you *pass*. Be sure you understand this difference.

DUMPING

Dumping, remember, is playing three or four bad letters for a limited score, in order to draw to a decent rack. With luck, you will end up with a good rack.

General guidelines are:

1. You must score in the neighborhood of one-half of your average, plus you must keep good letters. If your average play is 30 points, you would need to get 15 points or so on a dumping play.
   EIIHPRW. If you could play WHIP(EIR) for 15 points, it would be acceptable since you are keeping good letters.
   HIPUUVW. If you play WHIP(UUV) for 15, you keep crummy letters. Pass all seven.

2. When *dumping*, the letters you keep must be good and flexible. They don't have to be as good as the letters you keep when you *pass*, but they do have to have some positive value.
   The discussion on good letters to hold will be very useful in determining whether to pass or to dump.

Any three- or four-letter nonduplicated letters from RATES would be good. Any three or four letters from ADEILNRST are fine as long as they are flexible. ING would be fine to keep when dumping. It just isn't good enough to keep when passing.

For example, GIINNVY. If you can play VINY(ING) and get 15 points, that would be fine. It's reasonable to keep ING when you also get a decent score. *But*, with CCGINNY, it would be foolish to pass CCNY in order to keep ING. It's not good enough to keep if you also get no points. Pass all seven.

Big letters are not automatically good. You might decide to pass rather than to play and hold on to some high-point collection.

EEGGJKV. The word JEE(GGKV) for 12 points might not be worth playing.

AEEEJRS. The word JEE(AERS) for 12 would be good because of the fine letters you are keeping.

The important thing is to consider how well your remaining letters combine, not how many points they happen to be worth.

CEMTQUW. CWM(QUET) for 13 to 16 points would be acceptable. Note that QUET is a pretty good combination to keep. Anytime you have the Q and U, you can be optimistic. The ET makes it all the better.

CWM is an exceptional word for obvious reasons. It is a deep basin. Not many people know this one. If you can play it, the reaction you get will be worth it.

FISHING

Fishing is a little dangerous, in that you don't score much, if at all, and if you fail to draw good tiles, you will have the same problems you started with.

General rules on fishing are:

1. When you fish, you must be looking for a bingo or for a high-scoring play. Also, you must have a place to play if you draw well.

2. You should have a decent chance of drawing a good letter. If you are drawing one letter to AEIRST, there are eighteen letters that will give you a bingo. These letters represent eighty-one of the one hundred tiles in the game. Similarly, if you draw one letter to BGILLN, you will need a vowel for BALLING, BELLING, BILLING, BOLLING, or BULLING. There are forty-two vowels to draw out of one hundred tiles.

   You should not draw one letter to CIKLQY, hoping for a U to make QUICKLY. Hard to imagine doing this.

3. You must consider the score of the game as well as the points you can score if you just take your best play. For instance, if you are

leading, you should probably not fish. If you fish and miss, your opponent may improve his position. There's no need to kill your opponent. It's sufficient that you just beat him.

If you are trailing by 50 points, you might fish. But it would be silly to do so if you could score 40 points. Why give up enough points to tie up the game in search of a "maybe" bingo?

4. If the score is even, it is okay to fish, but you should not do so if you have a better than average play available.

BOARD MANAGEMENT

Picture these three scenarios:

1. You are leading comfortably. Suddenly, your opponent strikes with two bingos and your enormous lead shrinks to a small deficit.

2. You are trailing by a bunch. But good fortune comes your way and you draw a nice bingo. But you can't play it. So you make some compromise play and fortune stays with you. Sort of. You get another bingo, but still with no place to play.

3. In a tight game, your opponent manages to double-cross the J on a TLS and scores 61 points, the near equivalent of a bingo. Two plays later you draw the X and set out to recoup part of the new deficit. But luck is not with you. There is no way to play it for more than a minimum return.

Was this just bad luck?

To some extent, it was bad luck. But to some extent, it may have been a case of your opponent making a little luck for himself. It's called *board management.*

Board management is exactly what it sounds like. You literally manage the board to cater to your rack or to impede your opponent's needs.

Here are some possibilities:

Case 1. You are leading by 70 points and the only way you can lose is to have your opponent play a bingo.

What should you do?

In diagram 70, you have a 70-point lead and it's your turn. What should your thinking be?

E H L L M O W

Find a play that blocks your opponent's bingo lines.

DIAGRAM 70

With over sixty letters played (sixty-three), the game is quite advanced. Barring some strong Q or Z play, your opponent will need a bingo to win. Since the two blanks are still out, the chances of his getting one are relatively good.

With this in mind, you should consider impeding your opponent's ease of play. In other words, you want to block his bingo lines.

In diagram 70, you can choose from a variety of medium-scoring offensive plays, or you can play defensively.

Offensively, you have:

HELLO(MW)	at 15-F	27 points
HEW(LLMO)	at 2-J	30 points
OH(ELLMW)	at B-5	30 points
HOME(LLW)	at 2-H	32 points

Defensively, you would look for a play that would destroy potential bingo lines. Places where your opponent can play a bingo are:

1. **15-D–J**—A seven-letter bingo ending in O is possible.

2. **10-D–K**—An eight-letter bingo ending in R.

3. **D-8–15**—An eight-letter bingo starting with O.

4. **E-6–15**—An eight-letter bingo with an L as the first, second, or third letter.

5. **F-5–15**—An eight-letter bingo with an A as the first, second, third, or fourth letter.

6. **G-8–15**—An eight-letter bingo starting with C.

7. **3-A–J**—A ten-letter bingo using TOR, i.e., EXTORTIONS. Rather unlikely.

Obviously, it is impossible to find a play that blocks all these bingo lines, and that doesn't open up new ones. There is a play, however, that does block five of these bingo lines while giving away no new ones.

HOW(ELLM) at **9-D** is worth 21 points.

Look how it affects your opponent's possible plays. It blocks the "D," "E," "F," and "G" columns. And it blocks the 10 row. It is just as effective a block being played *next* to the 10 row as it would be if played *in* the 10 row.

Now the question arises whether you should give up 11 points for a tactical benefit.

You should. By blocking the bingo lines, you reduce your opponent's potential for a big play. If you lose 11 points and by doing so deprive your opponent of a bingo, your net gain will be as much as 50 points.

If the game was close, you couldn't use this tactic, or you would be less aggressive in doing so. You still have to win if possible, and in a close game those 11 points could be the difference.

If you are behind, you should not be blocking bingo lines. They could be instrumental in your getting back in the game. Anyway, if you are trailing, you won't have to worry about blocking bingo lines because your opponent will be busy doing that himself.

Case 2. You are trailing by 70 points and are running out of time. In these circumstances, you have to hope for a big play or for a series of good plays. If you get good letters you may get some high-scoring plays. But that is the function of luck.

If you don't draw those letters, your best hope will lie in a bingo. And, of course, a place to play it.

Row labels (top to bottom): 1 2 3 4 5 6 7 8 9 10 11 12 13 14 15

Column labels: A B C D E F G H I J K L M N O

Board letters:
- Row 1: P₃ R₁ I₁ V₄ A₁ T₁ E₁ ... H₄
- Row 2: R₁ ... B₃ E₁
- Row 3: T₁ O₁ ... A₁ X₈
- Row 4: O₁ D₂ ... G₂ A₁ B₃ Y₄
- Row 5: P₃ ... E₁ ... E₁
- Row 6: I₁ ... N₁ ... D₂
- Row 7: C₃ ... W₄ A₁ D₂ I₁
- Row 8: S₁ O₁ L₁ A₁ C₃ E₁ D₂ ... T₁ O₁ N₁ E₁ D₂
- Row 9: M₃ O₁ W₄ ... U₁
- Row 10: R₁
- Row 11: E₁

E E E L S T T

What should you do if leading by 70 points? What should you do if trailing by 70 points?

DIAGRAM 71

In diagram 71, you have no immediate bingo. There are bingo lines in the "M," "N," and "O" columns and the 10, 11, and 12 rows, but you aren't ready to use them.

On the other hand, you don't want to lose them. Only if you had a 40- or 50-point play would you purposely cut down the available bingo lines.

The right play is OMELET(EST) at **D-8** for 16 points, creating four new bingo lines in rows 11, 12, 13, and 14. Your opponent may be able to close some, but he won't be able to close all of them. Also, your leave (EST) is excellent.

Something like STEEL(ET) at **12-K** for 20 points would get you a few more points, but it would open up the TWS at **15-O**, plus it would close all currently open bingo lines. And just for extras, it would squander an S for nothing (you may need it for a hook).

If, in diagram 71, you led by 70 points, STEEL at **12-K** would be a good play since it scores decently and at the same time closes the board.

DIAGRAM 72

A B H O M P X

How can you set up
a good X play?

You might lose some points to the TWS at **15-O**, but it won't be nearly as expensive as a bingo.

Case 3. You have a high-scoring letter but no useful premium space on which to use it.

When this happens, you may be able to provide yourself with one.

In diagram 72, two TWSs are open on the 15 row. But you can't use them. Also, you have the X, but with no strong scoring opportunity.

By playing HOBO(AMPX) at **E-5**, you score 18, plus you set up the TLS at **6-F**. If this space remains open, you can follow with PAX at **F-5** for 58 points.

The reason your play will work is that there are other good or better spaces on the board. Your opponent may suspect what you are doing, but he will still tend to take his best play, which rates to be elsewhere. Without the TWSs at **15-H** and **15-O** to tempt your opponent, he would surely use the space you just made available.

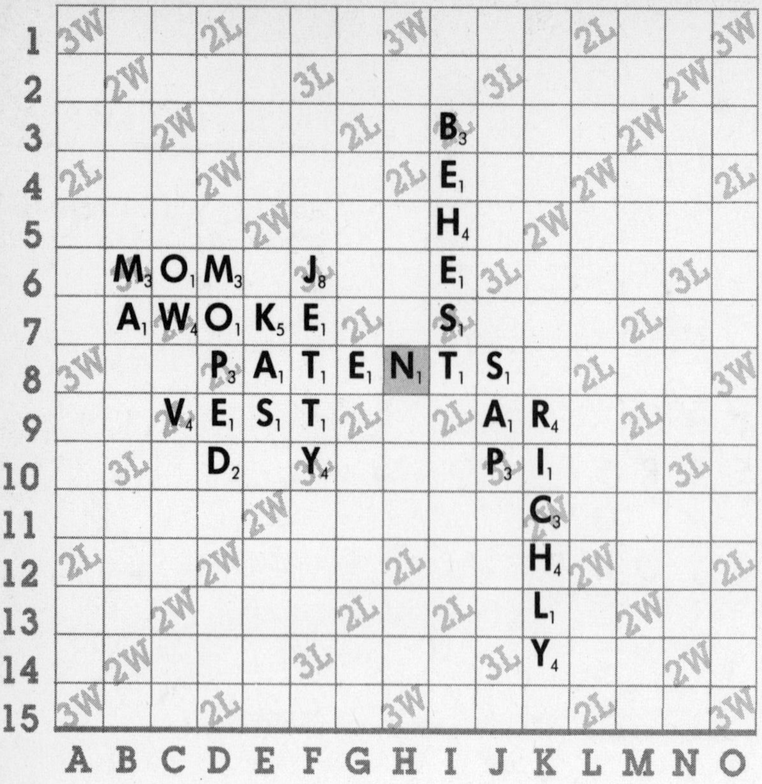

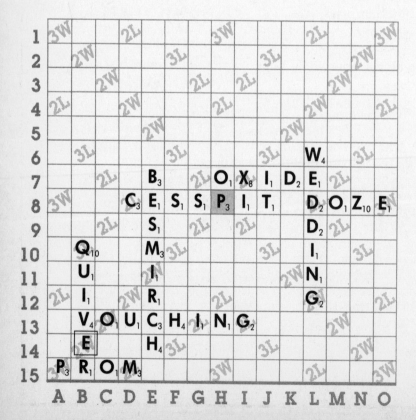

What is the hottest available space?

DIAGRAM 73

A E E K R S T

What letter should you fish and where?

DIAGRAM 74

Your opponent played HI.
What's up?

DIAGRAM 75

For instance, in diagram 73, your opponent just played BEHEST at **I-3**. Wouldn't you zoom in on the TLS at **6-J**? Regardless of your letters, you would spot **6-J** as the hottest space on the board and would use it if feasible.

Here are some more examples of opening up or of closing the board:

In diagram 74, you have a near bingo rack and you are trailing by 60 points. What should you play?

The K limits your flexibility. Fish it off at **J-6** for 17 points and hope for a bingo word. There's every chance this will work because you have an S. This will allow you to hook on to KIT(SKIT) giving you an unimpeded bingo row (5). Since eighteen letters will give you a bingo, the odds are heavily with you (ABCDFGHILMNOPRSTUW).

Even if you fish and fail, you might get lucky and be able to use the "O" column.

The essence of this play is that when you fish, you will often do so by playing one or two letters. You should try to make a play that will give you a place to play your bingo. Here, you played KIT, keeping your S for the hook.

In diagram 75, you opened with PRAWN and your opponent responded with HI. Smells fishy.

Your opponent is probably fishing for a bingo. It doesn't look like he's trying to set up the TLS at **10-B** because he can't double-cross it. It isn't worth making a 13-point play to set up a 30-point play. At least not this early in the game.

The sad thing about this rack is that you already have the bingo retakes. Unfortunately, you can't play it.

More likely, he is going for a bingo.

If he intends to hook on to HI with CHI, GHI, KHI, or PHI, good luck to him. But that's not going to happen. He is very unlikely to be fishing with a C, G, K, or P still on his rack.

More likely, he hopes to bingo on:
1. **10-D–J**—This requires a hook on to HI.
2. **The "I" column**—This requires an S to hook on to PRAWN.
3. **7-H–N**—This requires a hook on to the N.
4. **9-H–N**—This requires a hook on to the N.
5. Less likely, he may come up with an eight-letter bingo in the "E," "F," "G," or "H" columns using the A, W, or N in PRAWN.

Let's assume you have no good offensive play of your own, and that you decide to block. How should you do it?

Here are some plays and their effects on your opponent's bingo chances.

In diagram 76, you played TOUT.

This takes away the "F," "G," and "H" columns. If your opponent has a nine-letter bingo to play in "F," "G," or "H," that's just unlucky. TOUT leaves the 10 row intact, and since TOUT takes an S, it opens up the "J" column.

TOUT was not a good blocking word.

In diagram 77, we added REAP.

This play takes away columns "F," "G," and "H." It also takes away the "I" column and part of the 10 row.

It opens up the "J" column to an S hook and it opens up the right side of the 10 row.

REAP is a better block than TOUT was, but still is far from perfect.

Does TOUT block well?

DIAGRAM 76

Does REAP block well?

DIAGRAM 77

Why is OX a much better blocking play than TOUT or REAP?

DIAGRAM 78

In diagram 78, we used OX to block.

Even though OX is shorter than REAP or TOUT, it takes away the "G" and "H" columns. It takes away almost all of the 10 row (a few words will fit in, but not many). And, OX takes only one hook, OXY (containing oxygen).

OX is a much better defensive play than TOUT or REAP. Note again that one of its strengths defensively is that it doesn't take an S. Oftentimes it is necessary to know that a word does or does not take an S. To a lesser extent but still quite important is whether a word will take other hooks.

This concept will come up over and over, and everyone who plays much Scrabble® will begin to experience an automatic awareness of hooks.

On p. 220, you will find a list of two-letter words, along with each possible hook.

For example, the two-letter word AM takes hooks as follows:

Front Hooks	AM	Back Hooks
C	AM	A
D	AM	I
G	AM	P
H	AM	U
J	AM	
L	AM	
P	AM	
R	AM	
T	AM	
Y	AM	

This list will be worth your casual study.

SEVEN- AND EIGHT-LETTER WORDS

In the last four diagrams there was mention of seven-, eight-, nine-, and ten-letter bingos.

A seven-letter bingo is one that comes entirely from your rack and that is somehow hooked on to an already played word (unless it is the opening play).

An eight-, nine-, or ten-letter bingo is one that uses your seven letters, plus some number of previously played letters.

The reason this is important is that it is far easier to find a seven-letter bingo than an eight-letter or longer bingo.

When you are trying to block the board, you should concentrate first on places for a seven-letter bingo, then on places for longer ones.

RISK VERSUS GAIN

On p. 133 we discussed the concept of setting up a TLS in order to make an X play.

At the same time, the danger was noted that your opponent might grab the spot you set up and use it to his advantage.

Almost every time you make a play, you will be involved in two things:

1. What does the play gain?
2. What does the play risk?

Risk versus *gain*: How do they compare?

Until you can define these terms, you can hardly compare them.

What are the elements of gain?

1. Points
2. Rack balance
3. Tile turnover
4. Opening the board
5. Closing the board
6. Setting up a premium space

What are the elements of risk?

1. Leaving your opponent with a good place to play (usually premium spaces)
2. Giving your opponent a place to play his Q or other premium tiles
3. Leaving bingo lines for your opponent when you should be blocking them
4. Opening new bingo lines when you shouldn't
5. Keeping a poor rack

It's difficult to determine the correct ratio of risk to gain because your needs vary from game to game, from turn to turn. What you require today isn't what you require tomorrow.

Let's say you are stuck in "Middle Somewhere" and the only way out is by bus. A one-way bus ticket costs $101 and you have $100. A kid offers to flip a nickel for his $1 against your $100. This isn't much of an offer, but if you want that bus ride bad enough, you might have to flip that nickel. Risk versus gain. You risk $100 to gain $1.

Take the reverse analogy. You are independently wealthy, comfortably retired with $5 million tucked away in tax-free bonds. Would you be willing to risk that $5 million on a coin flip if you could win $100 million? You're getting good odds. You risk $5 million to win $100 million on an even money bet. I wouldn't do it either!

Or, if you were an NFL quarterback, you wouldn't start the game with four long passes (including fourth down). But if you were trailing in the last ten seconds, you might.

Needs of the moment always determine your level of risk. If you need nothing, you should risk nothing. If you're hurting, you have to take chances.

BONUS SPACES

Remember the discussions earlier:

1. The opening play
2. Double-crossing
3. Hot spots
4. Setting up a premium space

All four of these discussions emphasized the scoring potential of TLSs and DLSs and how to take advantage of them.

Unfortunately, most new players and many experienced ones put their emphasis on TWSs and DWSs, and ignore the TLSs and DLSs.

That's a bit odd because I've seen these same players go to great pains to set up a TLS, and get a good subsequent score. And then, moments later, they set up another TLS by accident.

And they get killed when their opponents score big with a double-crossed X or J.

If you reflect on how powerful a double-crossed H, J, K, or X can be on a TLS, and how much effort you went to in order to set one up, you should appreciate that you don't go around setting them up willy-nilly.

In the discussion on opening play, we looked at the danger of setting up the DLSs surrounding the starting star.

In the same way, you should be concerned about the TLSs and the other DLSs as well.

Fortunately, the answer is the same, i.e., don't, when you have options, leave a vowel next to a TLS or a DLS.

In diagrams 79 and 80, the first play was OWN, and you have chosen to play TAME or TEAM at **E-8**. You should choose TAME because it

Compare diagrams
79 and 80.

DIAGRAM 79

Compare diagrams
79 and 80.

DIAGRAM 80

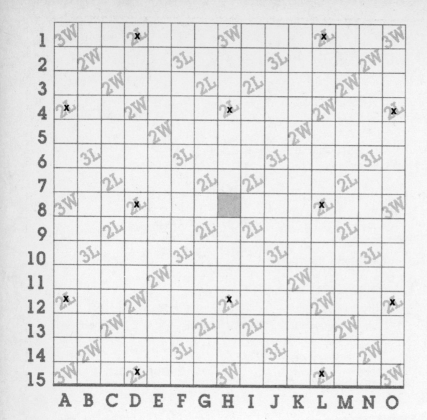

Why is it so dangerous to play a vowel next to one of the marked spaces?

DIAGRAM 81

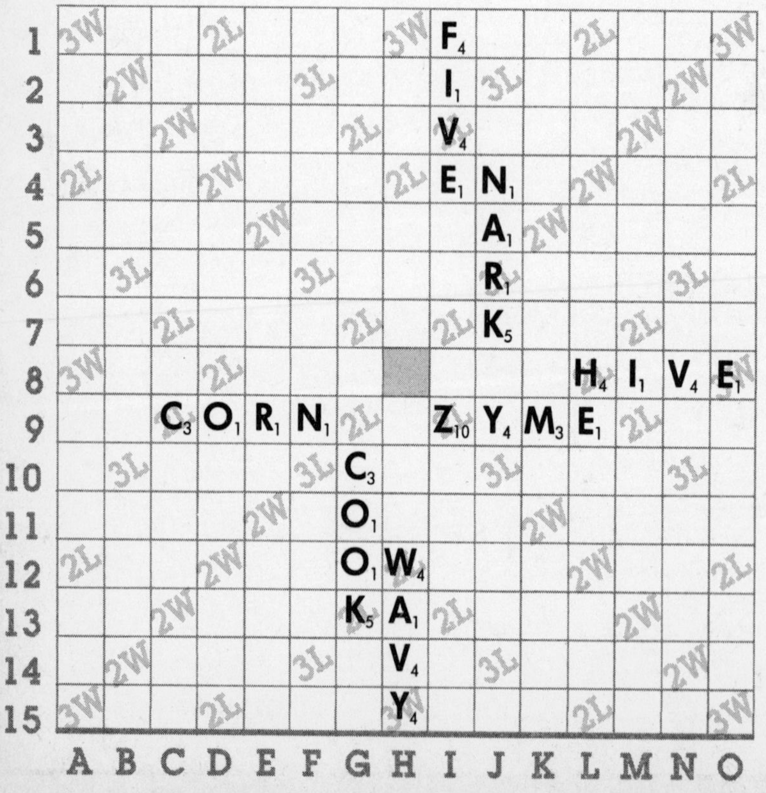

DIAGRAM 82

puts a consonant next to the TLS at **F-10**. It's better to put *any consonant* next to a DLS or TLS than a vowel.

You can prove this for your satisfaction by looking at the consequences of TAME versus TEAM.

In diagram 79, TAME was played, which put the M next to the TLS at **F-10**. AH at **F-10** is worth 18 points.

In diagram 80, TEAM was played, which put an A next to the TLS. HA at **F-10** is worth 30 points. Putting a vowel next to the TLS instead of a consonant lost you 12 points!

While you should be careful about exposing DLSs and TLSs, there are some that deserve special attention.

Note diagram 81. The twelve DLSs marked with a + are dangerous because they are near a TWS. If you leave a vowel next to one of these DLSs, it is an invitation to hook through the TWS.

In diagram 82, ZYME at **9-I** left an E next to the DLS. HIVE hooks on nicely and is worth 51 points.

NARK, at **I-4**, left a consonant next to the DLS but it was still expensive. FIVE at **H-1** is worth 36. The 15-point difference represents the cost to you of leaving a vowel rather than a consonant next to the DLS.

In the third example, CORN was played at **9-C**. It's okay to put the O next to the DLS at **8-D** because the C blocks access to the TWS.

You must be careful not to offer COOK at **G-10**. The K doesn't give the same protection that a C gives. WAVY hooks in there and is worth 66 points. Very expensive.

DOUBLE WORD SPACES (DWS)

Like any premium square you would like to use these yourself and deny them to your opponent.

There are a few things you can do with them to get best results.

For instance, when you have a choice of letters to place next to a DWS, you should put a low-scoring consonant next to it.

In diagram 83, there are three example situations:

Which is the most dangerous play?

DIAGRAM 83

---

1. The A in ART at **E-4** is next to the DWS. By adding EH at **D-3**, you score 20 points.

2. The R in RAT at **K-4** is next to the DWS. Adding HE at **L-3** is worth 14 points.

3. The M in MAT at **E-12** is next to the DWS. Adding HE at **D-11** is worth 18 points.

Note the enormous difference between playing a 1-point vowel and a 1-point consonant next to the DWS. It was more expensive to put the 1-point A next to a DWS than a 3-point M. Remember the discussion on exposing DLSs when you made your opening play? This is much the same.

TRIPLE WORD SPACES (TWS)

These are the most powerful premium spaces on the board. Most players are actively aware of them and don't expose them too freely. If anything, most players are overly cautious.

S A N D W I C H
F I S H
A C E D
B A T H
T O T
T A X
A B C D E F G H I J K L M N O

DIAGRAM 84

Because of their position on the board, it's usually easy to avoid contact with TWSs. It's also easy to open them up, but as long as you follow the approximate guidelines in this section, you should come out ahead.

EXPOSING OR OPENING UP A TWS

Let's say you are contemplating a play that will open up a TWS for your opponent. What should you get for such a play?

If points were your only consideration, you could use, as a guideline, that you don't want to expose a direct shot at a TWS unless you are gaining about 15 points over your next best play. If you are exposing an indirect shot at a TWS, you need to score about 8 points more than your next best play.

DIRECT SHOTS AND INDIRECT SHOTS

Sometimes you expose a TWS directly and sometimes you expose a TWS indirectly. Diagram 84 shows examples of both.

The S in SANDWICH (**E-1**) is in the 1 row, and thus it is directly in line with two TWSs. This is defined as directly exposing the TWS.

ACED at **11-B** and FISH at **4-K** provide indirect shots at a TWS. Your opponent will be able to reach a TWS only if he has letters that can hook on to ACED or FISH.

When a TWS can be reached only when you have a hooking letter, it is said to be indirectly exposed.

You might think it is more dangerous to leave a direct shot at a TWS than an indirect shot, but this is not always true.

In diagram 84 there are a variety of hooking situations.

The S in SANDWICH at **E-1** gives a direct shot at two TWSs. The greatest danger is that your opponent will be able to play an eight-letter bingo covering both TWSs. BIRDSEED at **1-A** would score 176 points. More likely, though, your opponent will play a five- or six-letter word going through one of the two TWSs. The score he gets will depend on whether he has useful high-scoring consonants. BACKS at **1-A** would score 54 points. If your opponent has poor letters he may not score well.

SHOOT at **1-E** would be worth 24 points and STOLE at **1-E** would be worth a mere 15 points.

The X in TAX at **C-13** also gives a direct shot at two TWSs. The danger of an eight-letter bingo is slight, but it does exist. These words will score a lot if your opponent can play one:

COXSWAIN	at **15-A**	239 points
DEXTROSE	at **15-A**	203 points
FIXATION	at **15-A**	221 points
FOXHOUND	at **15-A**	284 points
LAXATIVE	at **15-A**	221 points
MAXIMIZE	at **15-A**	311 points
SEXTUPLE	at **15-A**	212 points
SIXPENCE	at **15-A**	248 points
TAXATION	at **15-A**	194 points
VIXENISH	at **15-A**	248 points

In real life, your opponent will play something like this:

WAX	at **15-A**	39 points
WAXY	at **15-A**	63 points
TAXI	at **15-A**	36 points
MIXT	at **15-A**	42 points

As you can see, these small plays score very well. This is what happens when you leave a high-scoring letter on the TWS row that your opponent can capitalize on. The big letters may be hard to use, but when they are used, they pay well.

SIZE OF DANGER VERSUS FREQUENCY OF DANGER
OR
HOW EASILY CAN YOUR OPPONENT USE THE TWS?

What Hooks Are Available?

FISH at **4-K** in diagram 84 leaves an indirect shot at two TWSs. It's dangerous in that if your opponent has a Y, he will score a lot of points.

WARY	at **O-1**	60 points
YOURS	at **O-4**	54 points

The danger is limited in that FISH takes only a Y hook. If the two Y tiles and the two blanks have been played, your opponent won't be able to use the space.

ACED at **11-B** is another story. Whereas FISH took only a Y or a blank, ACED takes:

F + **ACED** = **FACED**	2 tiles
L + **ACED** = **LACED**	4 tiles
M + **ACED** = **MACED**	2 tiles
P + **ACED** = **PACED**	2 tiles
R + **ACED** = **RACED**	6 tiles

Counting the blanks, there are eighteen tiles that hook on to ACED.

If your opponent has a bingo containing F, L, M, P, or R, he may be able to hook it on to ACED. If he doesn't have a bingo, he is quite likely to have some sort of play in the "A" column.

FIGHT	at **A-11**	50 points
LAMED	at **A-11**	35 points
POUTS	at **A-11**	34 points
DREAM	at **A-7**	34 points
HOVER	at **A-7**	41 points
TUNER	at **A-7**	23 points

Even though hooking on to ACED scores less than hooking on to FISH, ACED is the more dangerous play because your opponent will probably be able to use it.

When you think in terms of hooks, you have to be aware of how many of each letter exist. TOT at **M-12** takes an E and an S (TOTE and TOTS) so you may be tempted to view it as safer than ACED, which took F, L, M, P, and R. When you counted the actual number of tiles that hooked on to ACED, it came to eighteen.

By comparison:

TOT + E = TOTE   there are 12 E tiles
TOT + S = TOTS   there are 4 S tiles

Adding the blanks, TOT and ACED have exactly the same number of hooking tiles, eighteen.

When leaving either direct or indirect shots at a TWS, you have to realize what your opponent's potential is.

This is determined by the combination of:

1. How much can he score?
2. How likely is that to occur?

Remember FISH and ACED in diagram 84?

FISH offered great points but was hard to use; ACED offered fewer points but was easier to use.

WHICH LETTERS SHOULD YOU LEAVE ON A TWS ROW?

When you make a play that leaves a letter in a TWS row, you should try, in general, to leave *inflexible* letters in the TWS row. *If* you leave letters like F, J, U, W, and Y, your opponent will have a tough time getting a really good play out of it. Although these tiles limit your opponent's responses, you could be hurt with such plays as LEFTY, MAJOR, UNPLUG, etc., if he has the right tiles. Remember also that it is more difficult to use a tile if it is 2 or 3 spaces away from a premium square, than if it is right next to it.

Letters like ADEILNRST are highly flexible and therefore highly dangerous for two reasons:

1. Your opponent may be able to make an eight-letter bingo.
2. Even if no bingo, these flexible letters will allow your opponent to get good mileage out of his rack.

In diagram 85, you can choose to play THRU at **F-12** or HURT at **10-L**. Since THRU leaves a U on the TWS row, it is far superior to HURT, which leaves a T. Of course, if your opponent replies with QUIZ, you will regret your decision.

One additional aside here. When you do leave a letter in a TWS row, the farther you can play it from the TWS, the harder it is for your opponent to use it.

Before presenting the dangers of leaving direct and indirect shots at a TWS, the question was asked, How many points should you gain in order to justify giving up a shot at a TWS?

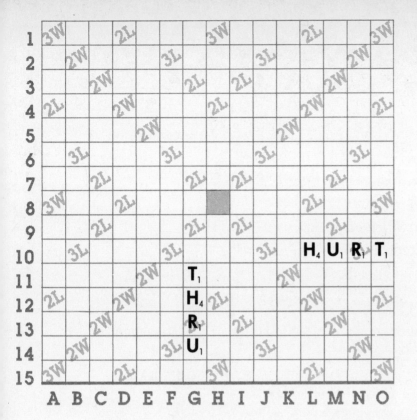

DIAGRAM 85

With an eye to the many variables and dangers discussed above, I repeat the following guidelines:

1. If you are leaving a *direct* shot at a TWS, you need to score 10 points more than your next best play.

2. If you are leaving an *indirect* shot at a TWS, you need to score 6 points more than your next best play.

I said before, and I say again, that these are approximate guidelines. You have to learn to estimate the dangers of the position and to adjust the guidelines appropriately.

Here's another example of hooks and their effect on your strategy. *Remember:* The more hooks your word has, the more dangerous it is. The more dangerous it is, the more your need to score to compensate. Be sure, when you make a dangerous play, how many hooking letters there are and how many of them are still in play.

In diagram 86, you can choose from:

HASTY(TU)	at **B-10**	47 points
SHAY(TTU)	at **M-10**	33 points
THY(ASTU)	at **8-A**	32 points

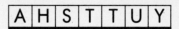

DIAGRAM 86

HASTY(TU) is clearly best. It does open the TWS at **8-A** but it does so indirectly. Your opponent will need an A, E, O, S, or ☐ to hook on to the H. Normally that would total thirty-five letters. There aren't that many high-scoring words ending in A or O, so the danger is not as great as it looks.

Since you are scoring 14 points more than your next best play, it's worth giving up an indirect shot.

Two asides here:

1. The TWS at **8-A** is already available to your opponent if he can play from **8-A** to **8-C** or **8-D**.

2. Some of the hooking letters (AEOS☐) have already been used. Ten have been played (five As, two Es, two Os, and one ☐) and you hold an A and an S in your rack. Always be aware of how many hooking letters *actually* remain in play.

Of the other two plays, THY(ASTU) is far superior to SHAY(TTU). THY scores 1 point less but it keeps your S and it also uses the TWS at **8-A**. You would not want to see your opponent play QUA or OXY at **8-A**.

B E E O O R S

Is it too risky to play OBOE(ERS) at **6-K**?

DIAGRAM 87

OTHER REASONS FOR EXPOSING BONUS SPACES

Keeping in mind the principle of risk versus gain, we can take a further look at strategies for bonus spaces.

There are quite a few reasons why you would open a premium space:

1. The first reason, which we looked at earlier, was that you hoped to use it on your next turn.

2. You may want to dump some letters. If it's sufficiently important to you to dump, you might risk opening up a premium space to do so.

   In diagram 87, you are trailing by 37 points. By dumping OBOE(ERS) at **6-K**, you get 15 points plus a good leave.

   If your opponent has the last blank or the last S, he can use the "O" column. But if he hasn't, you rate to do well.

   Note that in diagram 87, your play left an indirect shot at the triple-word column. Your opponent needs a specific tile to take advantage. In this case, an S or a ☐ was required.

153

How risky is
ORATE at **6-K**?

DIAGRAM 88

A I N N N O T

Should you play
NATION(N)
at **10-I** for 16 points,
or should you pass?

DIAGRAM 89

DIAGRAM 90

If, instead of OBOE, you had played ORATE, as in diagram 88, you would leave a direct shot at the "O" column. This obviously is far more dangerous.

3. In a similar fashion, you may wish to get rid of a maximum number of letters, going for turnover. In diagram 89, you have AINNNOT and a 7-point lead.

   With a clumsy assortment of letters and no good offensive play available, you might choose to pass seven letters.

   An alternative exists, which is to play NATION(N) at **10-I** for 16 points. This runs the risk of giving up a good score along the "O" column but it does get rid of six letters, which is a plus for you.

   Is it reasonable to take this risk?

   Yes. While your opponent may score well, he doesn't have to. Also, if he can't use this opportunity (no S or blank), you may be able to yourself.

   This brings up another concept:

   When you make a play, is what you gain more or less than what your opponent gains from your play?

DIAGRAM 91

In diagram 90, you played NATION for 16 points. Your opponent had an S and used it. FLAKES at **O-5** for 46 points.

By comparison, in diagram 91 you passed seven tiles. Your opponent, using the same word as in diagram 90, played FLAKES at **J-3** for 37 points.

When you played NOTION for 16 points, your opponent answered with FLAKES for 46 points. You lost 30 points on the exchange.

If you passed for zero points, your opponent would answer with FLAKES for 37 points. He scores 9 fewer points here, but his net for the turn is 37 points, or 7 points more than when you played NOTION.

4. The fourth reason for opening up a premium space is that you are making a high-scoring play. For example, if you have a bingo, you should almost always take the points even if it leaves good openings for your opponent.

It's difficult to say how many points you should get to justify this because there are so many variables. You will have to learn to judge the dangers as your experience and awareness develop. The discussion beginning on p. 146 will help illustrate your considerations.

Other factors include:

1. Am I ahead or behind?

2. How many premium letters are still out? Is it worth trying for turn-over in order to draw a useful tile?

3. How easily can my opponent benefit from my play?

4. Rack balance

STRATEGIES WHEN YOU HAVE A GOOD OR A BAD LEAVE

Remember when you last had a bingo but couldn't play it? Or when your opponent had one and there was a convenient place to play it?

Some of this was luck, but some was the result of good board management and anticipation.

It works this way:

When you can keep bingo-prone letters in your rack, you should try to play words that leave openings. For instance, if your opening rack is CDELOUS you can choose from COULD(ES) or CLOUD(ES). These both score the same and they keep the same letters (ES). If you decide there is nothing better, you should choose CLOUD.

With excellent letters to draw to, you have bingo chances, plus you have an S. If you get your bingo, you may be able to tack your word onto CLOUD.

If you had played COULD you might find it difficult to play a bingo if you got one.

If your opening rack was CCDLOUP you would be better off starting with COULD(CP). The (CP) leave doesn't promise much chance of a bingo, so you should not wish to open up the board.

This concept can apply throughout the game. Anytime you are drawing to bingo-prone letters (see p. 107), you should try to leave yourself a place to play it if you get it.

Conversely, when you have no expectation of a bingo, you should play words that restrict bingo possibilities.

Hot Spots

An occasionally exasperating moment is when there is an incredibly inviting place to play and you just can't use it.

In diagram 92, the "O" column looks awfully good. Perhaps you can get a *triple-triple* bingo. Something as simple as INTERNAL at **O-1** would be worth 122 points, and something a little richer, like EXPELLED, at **O-1** would be worth 212.

Unfortunately, your rack is DEEIUS ☐. There is no playable bingo here and no good score either.

Should you play, say, SID*E*(EEU ☐) at **O-1** for 15 points? At least you would deprive your opponent of a good spot to play.

No. Much better would be to play DUE (EIS ☐) at **10-A** for 10 points. This leaves you with an extremely good rack, plus a guaranteed good place to play. Either the "A" or "O" column will be available.

With your EIS ☐, you have super chances of a bingo. True, your opponent may have a good play on this turn, but you will have a better play more times than not.

In comparison, if you play SID*E*(EEU ☐) at **O-1**, you don't keep as good a rack. You waste your S and your ensuing play won't be as dynamic.

The rule here is: If the board has one hot spot and you can't use it, then you should make another one. The chances are you will get a good play next time.

There is a common error made in this situation. If there is a hot spot, say a TWS, and you have poor letters, the one thing you should not do is to block the TWS if you get both a poor score and a poor leave.

DEEIUS□

Should you block the "O" column?

DIAGRAM 92

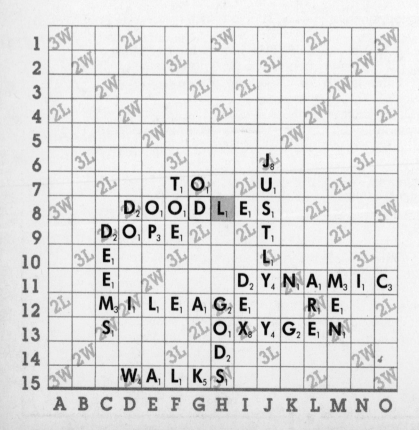

ANOSTV□

When would it be right to play AV*E*(NOST□) at **10-A**? When would it be right to play *CANTO*(SV□) at **O-11**?

DIAGRAM 93

Much better to pass seven letters and let your opponent have the hot spot.

Remember, he may not be able to use it effectively either. Even if he can use it, you may come out ahead. If you block the hot spot and keep bad letters, you may end up with two or three low-scoring turns.

By passing, you hope your subsequent plays will make up for whatever happens on the current turn.

Always consider future turns as well as the present turn.

A corollary to this is: If the board has two hot spots and you can't benefit from either, then play elsewhere and leave both of them open. *Do not* use one of the hot spots for a little score just to block it. Another fairly common error in this situation is for a player not only to block a hot spot but to do so with his good letters. This nets both few points and a poor rack. Not good tactics!

In diagram 93, you have a similar position. Should you use the TWS at **O-15**, CANTO(SV☐) at **O-11** for 24 points, or should you open the board by playing AV*E*(NOST☐) at **10-E** for 14 points?

Your play should be based on the score. If you were trailing by 70 or more, you should play AVE at **10-E** and hope for a huge play on your next turn.

If you were trailing by less than 70, or if you were ahead, the right play would be *C*ANTO at **O-11** for 24 points. If the game is not out of hand, there is no need to open the board dangerously. One major difference between this position and the previous position is that you can get a nice score (24 points) without hurting your rack. SV☐ is good. You keep two of the most important letters (S☐), so your bingo potential remains intact.

The reason why trailing by 70 points is important is that bingos are worth, on the average, about 70 points. When you fall behind by more than a bingo, you should start to think aggressively. But until you are behind by 70 points, or until late in the game, you don't want to offer your opponent too many chances. Give luck a chance until the situation is genuinely hopeless.

THE END GAME

In various places in this book, there have been some references to dangers in the late stage of the game. Specifically mentioned was the danger of being caught with some high-point letters when your opponent "goes out."

What was not mentioned was what you should do to avoid being caught.

Remember, when your opponent goes out, he gets two times the value of your remaining letters. That's the equivalent of using all your letters on a DWS. If your last letters are AFIQ, you lose 32 points. Easy enough to turn a winning game into a losing game.

What you should do is quite simple. When the game gets near the end, you should make a point of getting rid of your high-point letters, *even* if it costs you a few points to do so.

All this strategy requires is that you be aware of how many letters remain. And then play accordingly.

In diagram 94, you are leading by 5 points, with JKES left to play. Your opponent has two tiles, and if you have been paying attention to the major tiles, you know he has the remaining blank.

There are two pretty good plays available. *HEXES*(JK) at **5-H** is worth 36 points, and *JOKE*(S) at **L-7** is worth 15 points.

If you decide to choose from one of these plays, which would it be, and why?

Normally, you would take the 36 points, but end-game considerations suggest you take the 15 points from JOKE. Your opponent is surely going out on his next play, and is going to score a penalty bonus from your leftover letters.

J	K	E	S			

Your opponent is going out on his next turn. Should you play: *HEXES* (**5-H**) for 36 points or *JOKE* (**L-7**) for 15 points?

What should you play?

DIAGRAM 94

If you play HEXES, you will score 36 points, but will suffer a 26-point penalty from still having the J and K. The net to you will be only 10 points. If you play JOKE, you get only 15 points, but the penalty against you will be 2 points only, for a net of 13.

JOKE, therefore, is 3 points better than HEXES in spite of the fact that HEXES scores 21 points more.

There's another way of looking at this. When you played the J, you effectively got three times its value. You got 8 points for playing it and you saved 16 points by not being caught with it.

Don't overlook the cost of being stuck with a premium letter.

Q STRATEGIES

One of the easiest and most painful ways to lose a game of Scrabble® is to end up being stuck with the Q and the 20-point penalty that goes with it.

No matter what you do, it's going to happen to you sooner or later, but there's no reason you have to make a habit of eating the Q. By following a few simple guidelines, you should be able to avoid a penalty Q, and with luck you may be able to stick it on your opponent.

There are a number of different situations and we will look at each of them.

First, what do you do when you have the Q?

Case 1. End game. You have the Q and there is a place to play it.

Usually, you will be right to play it even if you have a higher-scoring play available. There are, of course, exceptions:

1. If you can score 30 *more* points elsewhere, take the points.

2. If there are two places to play the Q, and if you will get another turn, it is okay to make a higher-scoring play even if only a few points better. As long as you know you can play the Q on a later turn, there is less urgency to do so now.

Case 2. End game. You have the Q plus a U, but no place to play.

When this happens, you should try to set up a place to play the Q. One problem with this is that your opponent may suspect what you are doing and meanly block your play.

How can he tell you have the Q?

One way, of course, is that all the tiles have been taken and he knows you have it.

Another way is for you to have complained or in some other manner informed him that you have it. Letting your opponent know you have the Q is a huge giveaway. Not only does he know you are in trouble, but he also knows:

1. You are unlikely to have a bingo.

2. He won't draw the Q himself (at least not until you put it back!). And, he can afford certain plays he otherwise could not risk.

The only thing worse than having a Q headache is letting your opponent know it. This is especially true when there are six or fewer tiles in the bag. If your opponent knows you have the Q, *and can no longer pass it back*, you are in trouble.

Returning to the strategy of creating places to play your Q: On occasion, you may be able to set up two places to play it. This is important since it will be hard for your opponent to block both of them.

A A E P Q T U

Why is APNEA at
12-J correct?

DIAGRAM 95

In diagram 95, you have AAEPQTU. APNEA(QTU), at **12-J**, does nicely.
You intend to play QUA at **J-10** or **N-10** for 32 points on your next turn.

*Case 3. End game. You have the Q but no U, plus there are seven or
more letters left and you can still pass.*

Very likely, you should pass the Q. Certainly you should pass it if getting stuck with it means you will lose the game.

You would not pass it if you were able to score enough points to make
up for getting caught. Recognize that the penalty for getting caught
with the Q is twofold. There is a visible penalty and an invisible penalty.

The visible penalty is 20 points. The invisible penalty is that your opponent will profit by knowing you will be caught with the Q.

Remember that passing the Q is not a surefire cure. Sometimes you get
it back! You should not pass the Q if you think you can afford to eat it.
If you pass it, you lose a scoring turn. If you get the Q back, you lose a
turn, plus you still lose the 20 points.

DIAGRAM 96

DEEQSTW

Your opponent is down to six tiles. Should you make your highest-scoring play (WASTED(EQ) at **9-G** for 26 points)?

If you do choose to pass, you should pass most or all of your letters if there are U tiles or blanks left. Maybe you can draw one, in which case you will be prepared for the Q if you get it back. If there are no U tiles or blanks, then you should keep letters that you expect you can use.

Case 4. End game. You have an unplayable Q and it is too late to pass it. In diagram 96, there are no letters in the bag. Your Q is unplayable and your opponent knows you have it.

Your highest-scoring play is WASTED(EQ) at **9-G** for 24 points. But it is not your best play.

If you make this play, you will be able to play your E on the next turn, but thereafter you will have to sit and do nothing while your opponent takes his turns.

What he will do, therefore, will be to take many turns using one letter at a time, scoring 6 or 7 points per turn. Since he has six letters left, his potential is around 40 points. Far more than he could get by playing them all at once.

Look again at diagram 96. Note the various places for one-letter plays. CHAT at **E-10** plus an S is worth 10 points. BLOAT at **15-H** plus an S is worth 7 points.

AY at **J-1** + **E**,	6 points (AYE)
HIN at **6-J** + **D**,	12 points (HIND + RED)
A at **C-6** + **H**,	9 points (AH)
I at **13-H** + **F**,	9 points (IF)
E at **C-3** + **B**,	8 points (BE + BI)
K at **D-8** + **A**,	6 points (KA)
I at **D-12** + **F**,	11 points (IF + EFT)
RE at **M-4** + **A, E, I, or O**	6 points (ARE, ERE, IRE, and ORE)

Enough examples. It is clear that there are sufficient opportunities that your opponent will be able to score a bunch, even if he does do it slowly. And then, to top it all off, he's going to get the 20-point bonus from you at the end. Something to look forward to.

What you can do to circumvent this is rather curious. Fight fire with fire, as it were. You, too, should make little plays. Instead of playing WASTED, you should play WAD(EEQST) at **G-9** for 22 points. Now, when your opponent makes one-letter plays, you will be able to do so as well. Only nickel and dime plays, but you will share them rather than give them all to your opponent.

You'll be able to get three or four small plays, so the net to you will be somewhere around 25 points.

If your opponent does choose to go out, you won't be hurt too badly because you have already rid yourself of as many big-value letters as possible.

END STRATEGIES WHEN YOU DON'T HAVE THE Q

Case 5. End game. The Q has not been played and you don't have it, plus you have no U or blank.

In this case, you should play *little words* (one or two letters) so as to minimize your chances of drawing the Q.

How hard you pursue this strategy depends, of course, on the score. If you need points, you will have to take them at extra risk of drawing the Q.

Case 6. End game. The Q hasn't been played and you don't have it, plus you have a U or blank.

Hang on to the U or blank tile until the Q is gone or until you can end the game.

Again, if you need points, you may take them, but remember that if your opponent gets stuck with the Q, it's 20 points to you. If that's enough for you to win the game, you should be less quick to grab the points.

Case 7. End game. Your opponent has the Q and he can no longer pass it.

You should do two things:

1. If you see a place for your opponent to use the Q, you should block that spot. He will try to open spots on the board where he can play his Q. If he is able to open two spots at once, you may not be able to block both. But you should be able to block if he opens up a single spot.
   Be careful that you do not open up a spot yourself, by accident. Also, remember those special Q words that don't require a U (QAID is the most common word, but you shouldn't forget QOPH and FAQIR).

2. The second thing you should do when your opponent is stuck with the Q is to make lots of little plays. Don't take one big play. Take lots of small ones (see *case 4*). An exception to this, of course, is that if your opponent has high-point letters other than the Q, you should go out before he can get rid of them.

KEEPING TRACK OF THE LETTERS

A finer point of Scrabble® that should be practiced, to some degree, by everyone is the habit of keeping track of the letters as they are played.

Even when you play your first games of Scrabble®, you should be aware of how many blanks are left and whether the Q has been played. And, until the Q has been played, you should count the four U tiles. This will help you avoid being stuck with the Q and no U.

As your experience grows, you should keep an eye on the four S tiles. Eventually, you will know automatically which of the important letters have been played.

Even an awareness of the little letters can be important. For instance, if you had AEGIINT and had to choose from TIEING(A) or EATING(I), your decision would be influenced if you knew how many A tiles and I tiles had been played. If one A remained and six I tiles remained, you would know you were likely to draw an I. Therefore, your play would be TIEING(A), since you would be relatively unlikely to draw another A. If you played EATING(I), you would run the serious risk of ending up with duplicated I tiles.

Some players do this counting to the extreme that they make a note to themselves on their scorecard as each letter is played (it's legal). This is helpful but time-consuming.

I suggest a compromise in which you practice following the major letters. This knack will take a little time to develop, but after a while it will become second nature to you. The benefits will be quite worthwhile.

$\mathbf{Q}$UIZ FOR SECTION 2

1. Your opening rack is AAFIOVW. Which of these two plays do you choose?

   a. WAIF(AOV)   at **8-G**   20 points
   b. AVOW(AIF)   at **8-F**   20 points

2. Your opening rack is AIMTTTW. Which of these plays do you choose?

   a. TWIT(AMT)   at **8-F**   14 points
   b. MITT(ATW)   at **8-G**   12 points
   c. MAW(ITTT)   at **8-G**   16 points

3. Your opening rack is AADPRY☐. Which of these plays do you choose?

   a. PAY(ADR☐)   at **8-G**   16 points
   b. YARD⑤(AP)   at **8-D**   24 points
   c. PRAY⑤(AD)   at **8-D**   24 points
   d. YARD(AP☐)   at **8-E**   16 points
   e. PRAY(AD☐)   at **8-F**   16 points

4. Your opening rack is AAEGSVW. Which of these plays do you choose?

   a. GAVE(ASW)   at **8-E**   16 points
   b. WAVE(AGS)   at **8-E**   20 points
   c. WAVES(AG)   at **8-D**   30 points

5. Your opening rack is AEOQRST. What is your play?

6. Your opening rack is AERSTVW. What do you play?

7. What is hooking?

8. What is important about the letter group RATES?

9. What is board management?

10. What should you do if you are way ahead in a game?

11. What should you do if you are way behind in a game?

12. Is it more dangerous to leave an X or an E next to a TLS?

13. What is the SATIRE list?

14. Which vowel can stand duplication and even triplication?

15. Which is the worst vowel for duplication?

16. If you have both blanks and you draw five new letters, are your chances of getting a bingo more or less than 50 percent?

17. What single letters can you hook to READ?

18. What is turnover? Why is it important?

19. How many points (generally speaking) must you get to justify giving your opponent a direct shot at a TWS?

20. Should you pass four letters to keep ING?

21. If you decide to dump, how many points must you score? What other condition is important?

22. Should you dump four letters if you are keeping ING?

23. If you expect your opponent is about to go out, should your only objective be to score points?

24. If your opponent is stuck with the Q and can't go out, what should you do?

25. Halfway through the game, one U and no blanks have been played. Should you pass the Q (in general)?

ANSWERS

1. **AAFIOVW**
   a. **AVOW(AIF)** 20 points. Best. It keeps relatively good letters.
   b. **WAIF(AOV)** 20 points. AO is a poor combination and should be avoided when possible.

2. **AIMTTTW**
   a. **TWIT(AMT)** 14 points. Best. It's important to break up that duplication of Ts. Also, WATT uses one more letter than MAW and thus gives better turnover.
   b. **MITT(ATW)** 12 points. Almost as good.
   c. **MAW(ITT)** 16 points. Even with the extra points, this is poor. It keeps TTT, which is awful.

3. **AADPRY☐**
   a. **PRAY(AD☐)** 18 points. Best. Don't use the blank for a small return. PRAY is the best-scoring play given you keep the ☐.
   b. **YARD(AP☐)** 16 points. Almost as good.
   c. **PAY(ADR☐)** 16 points. In general, you want to play long words so as to increase your chances of drawing premium tiles.

4. **AAEGSVW**
   a. **WAVES(AG)** 30 points. Best. Take the extra 10 points by using the S.
   b. **WAVE(AGS)** 20 points. False economy.
   c. **GAVE(ASW)** 16 points. (ASW) is not worth 4 points more than (AGS).

5. **AEOQRST**
   Pass **OQ(AERST)**. Keep exceptional letters. There was no good-scoring play available, so you lose little by passing.

6. **AERSTVW**
   WAVER(ST) at **8-D** for 30 points. You get a good score and a good leave so you should not consider passing as in problem 5, above.

7. Hooking is adding a letter to a previously played word, thus making a new word.

8. Keep your eyes open for this combination of letters in your rack! Any combination of letters from the group RATES is excellent to draw to, because they combine well to form words of many lengths, including bingos.

9. Board management is manipulating the board to fit your needs.

10. When you are way ahead in the game, you should cut down on the available bingo lines so your opponent won't be able to play a bingo if he gets one.

11. When you are way behind in a game, you should try to open up the board so that you will be able to play a bingo when you get it.

12. It is much more dangerous to leave an E next to a TLS than an X. (See p. 146.) Vowels are dangerous becuse they allow your opponent to double-cross high-scoring consonants.

13. The SATIRE list is a list of which letters, when added to SATIRE, make a bingo. Eighteen letters make bingos, eight don't.
    The SATIRE list and nine other lists can be found in the For the Curious section following this quiz.

14. You can easily use two E tiles and sometimes three.

15. Two U tiles are very poor.

16. You have an 80 percent chance of getting a bingo when you draw five letters to the two blanks.

17. The following letters can be hooked to READ:
    B, D, and T are front hooks for READ.
    D, S, and Y are back hooks for READ.

18. Turnover is playing as many letters as is safe so that you have extra chances of drawing the premium letters, i.e., X, S, blank, and in some situations the Z.

19. If you give a direct shot at a TWS, your play must be worth 10 points more than your second-best play.

20. ING is not worth passing for. It is a good ending, but not so good for making bingos.

21. If you dump, you should score at least half of your average turn. Also, you should be able to keep good flexible letters. Why dump if your rack has no future?

22. It is reasonable to dump, keeping ING, as long as you get decent points. Compare with answers 20 and 21.

23. On your final turn, you should consider playing your high-point letters. Even if you sacrifice points, you may come out ahead. Not losing penalty points is just as important as scoring points.

24. When your opponent can't play his Q in the end game, you should play your letters one at a time. Four or five 7-point plays are worth more than two 10-point plays.

   Do be careful not to give your opponent a place to play his Q.

25. With two blanks and three U tiles left in the bag, you should play and not pass.

QUIZ—ANAGRAMMING FOR BINGOS

Each of the following racks has one or more common bingos. The number in the center column indicates how many. How many can you find? As an aid you might want to set up a rack and move the tiles around.

Warning: Just because a word is relatively common doesn't mean it's easy to find. Remember those prefixes and suffixes!

1.	AADEGNS	(1)	AGENDAS
2.	AADEHIR	(1)	AIRHEAD
3.	AADEITW	(1)	AWAITED
4.	AADEMNT	(1)	MANDATE
5.	AADENRV	(1)	VERANDA
6.	AAEISTT	(1)	SATIATE
7.	AAENRRT	(1)	NARRATE
8.	AAENRUW	(1)	UNAWARE
9.	AALNRTU	(1)	NATURAL
10.	ABCEINT	(1)	CABINET
11.	ABCEIOT	(1)	ICEBOAT
12.	ABDEILS	(1)	DISABLE
13.	ABDEINR	(1)	BRAINED
14.	ABDEOST	(1)	BOASTED
15.	ABEELOR	(1)	EARLOBE
16.	ABEERST	(3)	BEATERS, REBATES, BERATES
17.	ABEGINR	(1)	BEARING
18.	ABEGINT	(1)	BEATING
19.	ABEINST	(1)	BASINET
20.	ABEIRTV	(1)	VIBRATE
21.	ABEMORT	(1)	BROMATE
22.	ABENOTY	(1)	BAYONET
23.	ABILORT	(1)	ORBITAL
24.	ABINOST	(3)	BONITAS, BASTION, OBTAINS
25.	ACDEENT	(1)	ENACTED
26.	ACDEINS	(2)	INCASED, CANDIES
27.	ACDENRS	(1)	DANCERS

28.	ACEELNR	(2)	RECLEAN, CLEANER
29.	ACEFINR	(1)	FANCIER
30.	ACEGINO	(1)	COINAGE
31.	ACEIRSU	(1)	SAUCIER
32.	ACLOORT	(1)	LOCATOR
33.	ACEMNOR	(1)	ROMANCE
34.	ACEORRT	(2)	CREATOR, REACTOR
35.	ACEORTU	(1)	OUTRACE
36.	ACEORTV	(1)	OVERACT
37.	ACGINOT	(1)	COATING
38.	ACINOTU	(2)	CAUTION, AUCTION
39.	ADDEIOR	(1)	RADIOED
40.	ADDENOT	(1)	DONATED
41.	ADEEFRT	(1)	DRAFTEE
42.	ADEEGNR	(5)	ANGERED, DERANGE, GRANDEE, GRENADE, ENRAGED
43.	ADEEGNT	(1)	NEGATED
44.	ADEEILM	(1)	LIMEADE
45.	ADEEIRS	(2)	DEARIES, READIES
46.	ADEEISS	(2)	DISEASE, SEASIDE
47.	ADEELNR	(1)	LEARNED
48.	ADEELRS	(2)	LEADERS, DEALERS
49.	ADEEOPT	(1)	ADOPTEE
50.	ADEFGOR	(1)	FORAGED
51.	ADEFINT	(2)	DEFIANT, FAINTED
52.	ADEGHIN	(1)	HEADING
53.	ADEGILN	(3)	ALIGNED, DEALING, LEADING
54.	ADEGNOR	(1)	GROANED
55.	ADEGNRT	(2)	DRAGNET, GRANTED
56.	ADEIIRS	(2)	DAIRIES, DIARIES
57.	ADEILST	(2)	DETAILS, DILATES
58.	ADEIMRT	(1)	READMIT
59.	ADEIMST	(1)	MISDATE
60.	ADEINRR	(1)	DRAINER
61.	ADEINRT	(2)	TRAINED, DETRAIN
62.	ADEIPRS	(4)	ASPIRED, DESPAIR, DIAPERS, PRAISED
63.	ADELORS	(3)	RELOADS, ORDEALS, LOADERS
64.	ADENOST	(1)	DONATES
65.	ADENPRU	(1)	UNDRAPE
66.	ADEMNOR	(1)	MADRONE
67.	ADEMRST	(1)	SMARTED
68.	ADENOST	(1)	DONATES
69.	ADEORSU	(1)	AROUSED
70.	ADERRST	(4)	DARTERS, RETARDS, STARRED, TRADERS
71.	ADGINRT	(2)	TRADING, DARTING
72.	ADIORTU	(1)	AUDITOR
73.	AEEELRS	(1)	RELEASE
74.	AEEGNRS	(1)	ENRAGES

75.	**AEEGNRV**	(2)	ENGRAVE, AVENGER
76.	**AEEGNST**	(1)	NEGATES
77.	**AEEHIRV**	(1)	HEAVIER
78.	**AEEHNRT**	(2)	HEARTEN, EARTHEN
79.	**AEEILNT**	(1)	LINEATE
80.	**AEEILRS**	(1)	REALISE
81.	**AEEILRZ**	(1)	REALIZE
82.	**AEEIMTT**	(1)	TEATIME
83.	**AEEIRRT**	(1)	TEARIER
84.	**AEEMNST**	(1)	MEANEST
85.	**AEENNTU**	(1)	UNEATEN
86.	**AEENRST**	(3)	EARNEST, EASTERN, NEAREST
87.	**AEENSTT**	(1)	NEATEST
88.	**AEEPRST**	(1)	REPEATS
89.	**AEEORTV**	(2)	OVEREAT, OVERATE
90.	**AEERSTW**	(1)	SWEATER
91.	**AEFGIRT**	(1)	FRIGATE
92.	**AEFIMNR**	(1)	FIREMAN
93.	**AEFINTR**	(1)	FAINTER
94.	**AEFIRTT**	(1)	FATTIER
95.	**AEFOPRN**	(1)	PROFANE
96.	**AEGIIMN**	(1)	IMAGINE
97.	**AEGILNP**	(2)	LEAPING, PEALING
98.	**AEGINOS**	(2)	AGONIES, AGONISE
99.	**AEGINRR**	(5)	ANGRIER, EARRING, RANGIER, REAR-ING, GRAINER
100.	**AEGINRT**	(4)	GRANITE, TEARING, INGRATE, TANGIER
101.	**AEGINTV**	(1)	VINTAGE
102.	**AEGLRST**	(1)	LARGEST
103.	**AEGNOTR**	(1)	NEGATOR
104.	**AEGORTU**	(1)	OUTRAGE
105.	**AEHILNS**	(1)	INHALES
106.	**AEHNORT**	(1)	ANOTHER
107.	**AEIINRT**	(1)	INERTIA
108.	**AEIIRST**	(1)	AIRIEST
109.	**AEIKNRS**	(1)	SNAKIER
110.	**AEILNOT**	(2)	TOENAIL, ELATION
111.	**AEILOST**	(1)	ISOLATE
112.	**AEINNRT**	(1)	ENTRAIN
113.	**AEINOSV**	(1)	EVASION
114.	**AEINRRT**	(3)	RETRAIN, TRAINER, TERRAIN
115.	**AEIORSV**	(1)	OVARIES
116.	**AEIPRTV**	(1)	PRIVATE
117.	**AEIRSST**	(1)	SATIRES
118.	**AEISTTU**	(1)	SITUATE
119.	**AELNNRT**	(1)	LANTERN
120.	**AELNPRT**	(2)	PLANTER, REPLANT
121.	**AELNRTU**	(1)	NEUTRAL

122.	**AELRSTT**	(3)	STARTLE, STARLET, RATTLES
123.	**AENORRV**	(1)	OVERRAN
124.	**AENRTVU**	(1)	VAUNTER
125.	**AEORSTT**	(2)	TOASTER, ROTATES
126.	**AGILNOT**	(1)	ANTILOG
127.	**AGINORT**	(1)	ORATING
128.	**AILRSTU**	(1)	RITUALS
129.	**AINORTU**	(1)	RAINOUT
130.	**AINOORT**	(1)	ORATION
131.	**BDEILOR**	(1)	BROILED
132.	**BEINRTU**	(2)	TRIBUNE, TURBINE
133.	**CDEEINO**	(1)	CODEINE
134.	**CEILORS**	(2)	RECOILS, COILERS
135.	**CEINOST**	(2)	SECTION, NOTICES
136.	**DEEEINR**	(1)	NEEDIER
137.	**DEEILOS**	(1)	OILSEED
138.	**DEEINNT**	(1)	DENTINE
139.	**DEEINTV**	(1)	EVIDENT
140.	**DEEIOPS**	(1)	EPISODE
141.	**DEEIRRT**	(3)	TIREDER, RETIRED, RETRIED
142.	**DEELNST**	(1)	NESTLED
143.	**DEELORS**	(1)	RESOLED
144.	**DEENORS**	(1)	ENDORSE
145.	**DEERNTU**	(3)	RETUNED, DENTURE, TENURED
146.	**DEEORTW**	(1)	TOWERED
147.	**DEFIOST**	(1)	FOISTED
148.	**DEGINOR**	(5)	NEGROID, ERODING, REDOING, IGNORED, GROINED
149.	**DEHIOTU**	(1)	HIDEOUT
150.	**DEIINOT**	(1)	EDITION
151.	**DEIINRS**	(1)	INSIDER
152.	**DEILOPT**	(1)	PILOTED
153.	**DEINNOT**	(1)	INTONED
154.	**DEINPRT**	(1)	PRINTED
155.	**DEINRTT**	(1)	TRIDENT
156.	**DEIOORW**	(1)	WOODIER
157.	**DEIINOS**	(2)	IONISED, IODINES
158.	**DEIORSW**	(3)	WEIRDOS, DOWRIES, ROWDIES
159.	**DEIOSTU**	(2)	OUTSIDE, TEDIOUS
160.	**DEIRSTU**	(2)	STUDIER, DUSTIER
161.	**DELORST**	(1)	OLDSTER
162.	**DELOSTU**	(2)	TOUSLED, LOUDEST
163.	**DENORST**	(2)	RODENTS, SNORTED
164.	**DEOORST**	(1)	ROOSTED
165.	**EEEIRST**	(1)	EERIEST
166.	**EEGILNT**	(1)	GENTILE
167.	**EEGIMNR**	(1)	REGIMEN
168.	**EEHINOR**	(1)	HEROINE
169.	**EEHINRT**	(2)	NEITHER, THEREIN

170. **EEIMNOT**	(1)	ONETIME
171. **EEINOPR**	(1)	PIONEER
172. **EEINRTU**	(3)	REUNITE, UTERINE, RETINUE
173. **EEIRSTT**	(1)	TESTIER
174. **AEEINRT**	(2)	TRAINEE, RETINAE
175. **EFGINOR**	(1)	FOREIGN
176. **EFIINTR**	(1)	NIFTIER
177. **EFINNOR**	(1)	INFERNO
178. **EGINRST**	(2)	STINGER, RESTING
179. **EGINRSU**	(1)	REUSING
180. **EGIOORS**	(1)	GOOSIER
181. **EGIRSTU**	(2)	GUTSIER, GUSTIER
182. **EHINRST**	(1)	HINTERS
183. **EHNORST**	(3)	THRONES, HORNETS, SHORTEN
184. **EIINNRT**	(1)	TINNIER
185. **EIINORS**	(2)	IRONIES, NOISIER
186. **EIINSTU**	(1)	UNITIES
187. **EILNOOR**	(1)	LOONIER
188. **EILNRST**	(1)	LINTERS
189. **EILOORS**	(1)	ORIOLES
190. **EINNORU**	(1)	REUNION
191. **EINOORS**	(1)	EROSION
192. **EINORTU**	(1)	ROUTINE
193. **EINRSTT**	(3)	RETINTS, TINTERS, STINTER
194. **EINRTTU**	(1)	NUTTIER
195. **EIOOPST**	(1)	ISOTOPE
196. **EIOORST**	(1)	SOOTIER
197. **EORRSTU**	(4)	ROUTERS, TROUSER, ROUSTER, TOURERS
198. **GINOORT**	(1)	ROOTING
199. **IILNORS**	(1)	SIRLOIN
200. **ILNOOST**	(1)	LOTIONS

SECTION

THREE

(Games)

The following two games are real games that were played by tournament players.

Game 1 was played by two solid, but not quite expert, players who made a predictable number of errors.

Game 2 was played by two of the country's top players. Even so, their plays were not always best. One or two difficult bingos were missed. Generally speaking, though, the level of play was high.

As an aid you might want to get your board out and play along.

TURN 1.
You go first with **A E I M O O V**

1. Do you have a bingo?
2. If no bingo, what should your goals be with this rack?
3. Choose from these plays:

a. VIM(AEOO)	**8-G**	16 points		**d.** MOVIE(AO)	**8-G**	20 points
b. MOVE(AIO)	**8-E**	18 points		**e.** AVE(IMOO)	**8-G**	12 points
c. MOVIE(AO)	**8-D**	26 points		**f.** OVA(EIMO)	**8-G**	12 points

ANSWERS:

1. You have no bingo.
2. Your goals should be:
    a. To break up your duplicated O tiles
    b. To put the M or V on a DLS at **8-D** or **8-L**
    c. To make as long a word as possible (turnover)
    d. To avoid putting a vowel next to a DLS; in this case, starting at **8-D** was worth 6 additional points, which compensated for the placement
3. The best play is MOVIE(AO) at **8-D**. It gives you the highest score, the most turnover, and it breaks up the double O tiles. The only bad thing about it is that it keeps AO. This is a slightly poor set of vowels.

    Your opponent replies with FRY at **9-G** for 28 points. He was able to use those DLSs to good advantage. The double-crossed F contributes 16 points by itself.

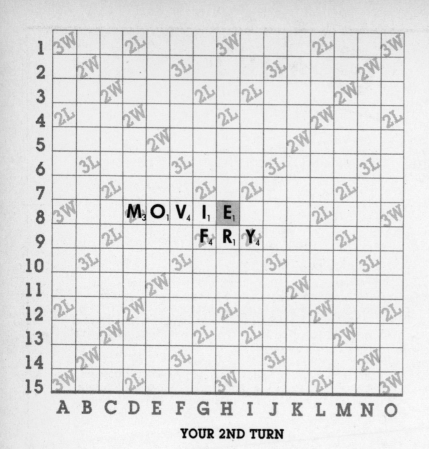

A G I N N N O

Opponent's last play—
FRY at **9-G**
28 points

SCORE: You   Opp
              26   28

DIAGRAM 97

YOUR 2ND TURN

D E F N N S V

Opponent's last play—
HAREM at **7-H**
17 points

SCORE: You   Opp
              46   45

DIAGRAM 98

YOUR 3RD TURN

TURN 2.   A G I N N N O   SCORE: You   Opp

                                         26   28

1. Do you have a bingo?
2. If no bingo, what should your goals be with this rack?
3. Are there any useful hot spots?
4. Choose from these plays:

   a. NAG(IONN)   **7-C**   12 points   **d.** *FRYING*(ANNO)   **9-G**   13 points
   b. *MANNING*(O)   **D-8**   20 points   **e.** *M*OANING(N)   **D-8**   20 points
   c. GAIN(NNO)   **10-H**   16 points

ANSWERS:

1. You have no bingo.
2. Your goals should be:
   a. Get rid of at least two N tiles
   b. Turnover
3. **E-5** to **E-11** offers a double-DWS. DISOWNS, for example, would be worth 44 points.
4. The best play is *M*OANING(N) at **D-8**. It is better than *MANNING*(O) because it keeps an N, a more useful letter than an O. The other three choices are weak because they score less, they don't use as many letters, and because they keep duplication (NN).

     Your opponent plays HAREM at **7-H** for 17 points, which is surely not his best play. It opens up the TWS at **8-O** to a big play and it doesn't even score very well. It will be disappointing not to be able to use this spot.

     A much better play for your opponent would have been the obscure word HAME (part of a horse collar). HAME at **C-10** would have been worth 33 points and would have been far safer.

TURN 3.   D E F N N S V   SCORE: You   Opp

                                           46   45

1. Do you have a bingo?
2. If no bingo, what should your goal be with this rack?
3. Are there any useful hot spots?
4. Choose from these plays:

   a. VENDS(NF)   **M-3**   32 points
   b. FENDS(NV)   **8-K**   40 points
   c. VE*N*D(FNNS)   **13-B**   16 points

ANSWERS:

1. You have no bingo.
2. To get rid of as many inflexible letters as possible. This rack is a long way from being balanced.
3. There are many good hot spots here:
   a. The TWS at **8-O**   **c.** **13-C** to **13-G** for a DLS and a DWS
   b. **K-5** to **K-11** for a double DWS   **d.** **14-B** to **14-F** for a DLS and a TLS
4. The best play is FENDS(NV) at **8-K** for 40 points. The highest-scoring play is often the right play. FENDS scores a healthy 8 points more than the next best play.

     Your opponent plays WHALE*R* at **J-2** for 22 points.

E N R T V Y □

Opponent's last play—
WHALER at **J-2**
22 points

SCORE: You   Opp
       86   67

DIAGRAM 99

YOUR 4TH TURN

E E N R T Z □

Opponent's last play—
TAXI at **C-10**
39 points

SCORE: You   Opp
       106   106

DIAGRAM 100

YOUR 5TH TURN

TURN 4.   **E N R T V Y** ☐   SCORE: You   Opp
                                               86   67

1. Do you have a bingo?
2. If no bingo, what should your goal be with this rack?
3. Are there any useful hot spots?
4. Does WHALER take a hook?
5. Choose from these plays:
    a. VARY(ENT☐)   **4-I**   20 points
    b. NAVY(ERT☐)   **10-C**   18 points
    c. NAVY(ERT☐)   **4-I**   20 points

ANSWERS:

1. You have no bingo. (As frequently seems to be the case, an obscure bingo was discovered during the postgame discussion. INVER☐TY at **12-D** was available.)
2. You are still trying to develop your rack. You are close, but still not quite yet ready to bingo. Get rid of, if possible, the VY combination.
3. This is a wide open board and it offers many opportunities. Hot spots include:
    a. 3-I to **3-M** for a DLS plus a DWS   **d.** Bingo chances in the "O" column
    b. 4-H to **4-L** for a DLS plus a DWS   **e. 13-C** to **13-G**
    c. 5-E to **5-K** for a double DWS   **f. 14-B** to **14-F**
4. WHALER doesn't take a front hook. It's very important, though, to consider hooks, no matter how silly they may seem.
5. The best play is NAVY(ERT☐) at **4-I**. This scores the same as VARY(ENT☐) at **4-I**, but it keeps ERT☐ instead of ENT☐. This is a small, but important, distinction. The big reason for not playing VARY is that it takes an O hook (OVARY). That would open the TWS at **1-H**!
    Your opponent comes back with TAXI at **C-10** for 39 points. Looks like a good play. It used four hooks, plus it shows an awareness of two-letter words. Nice.

TURN 5.   **E E N R T Z** ☐   SCORE: You   Opp
                                               106   106

1. Do you have a bingo?
2. If no bingo, what should your goal be for this rack?
3. Are there any useful hot spots?
4. Does NAVY take a front hook?
5. Choose from these plays:
    a. ZERO(ERT☐)   **E-5**   26 points
    b. ZE*D*(ERNT☐)   **N-6**   33 points

ANSWERS:

1. You have no bingo.
2. Try to get rid of the Z. EE is not a bad duplication to have, so it's not imperative to get rid of an E.
3. There are no special hot spots. Still keep an eye on the "O" column, though.
4. NAVY does not take a front hook.
5. ZE*D* is best. It scores nicely and keeps fine letters. The only fault with ZER*O* is that it scores 7 fewer points.
    Your opponent plays *GAWK* at **14-D** for 20 points. This is mildly dangerous, since he is giving you the TWS at **15-H**. The reason it's not terribly dangerous is that you need, specifically, an A to hook on to the K (KA) or an S to hook on to GAWK. Still, if you could play something like FISH at **H-12**, it would be worth 55 points. I imagine your opponent is trying, as you have been, to get rid of some awkward letters.

E E G N R T □

Opponent's last play—
GAWK at **14-D**
20 points

SCORE: You   Opp
        139   126

DIAGRAM 101

YOUR 6TH TURN

A A B O O Q T

Opponent's last play—
TEAR at **15-E**
25 points

SCORE: You   Opp
        216   151

DIAGRAM 102

YOUR 7TH TURN

TURN 6.   E E G N R T ☐   **SCORE:**   **You**   **Opp**
                                      139   126

1. Do you have a bingo?
2. If not, what should your goal be with this rack?
3. Are there any useful hot spots?
4. Would you consider playing:
     a. RE⬚S⬚T(EGN)   **H-12**   25 points; or
     b. NE⬚A⬚TER(G)   **15-E**   27 points

ANSWERS:

1. Yes, you have GENT⬚L⬚ER. Can you play it anywhere? Yes, GENT⬚L⬚ER at **B-5** equals 69 points. Is this your only bingo? You also have *STEER⬚I⬚ING* at **O-8** for 77 points.
2. If you didn't find the bingos, you would try to play the G and one or two other letters. Say TONG(EER⬚) at **E-7** for 11 points.
3. There are two hot spots: the TWS at **15-H** and the "O" column.
4. No. It would be a huge waste of the ☐ to take 25 or 27 points.
     Note that if you found either bingo, you looked for another. Also notice that finding STEERING required you to look further than your rack. Being aware that there was scoring potential in the "O" column was a big help because it caused you to look for a bingo beginning with S. Let the hot spots help you find good plays. You have to pay attention at all times both to your rack and to the letters and hot spots on the board.
     Your opponent plays TEAR at **15-E** for 25 points. Another play with multiple hooks.
     Oops! You've played too hastily. You missed TREE⬚I⬚NG and RE⬚A⬚GENT. You might not have been able to play TREE⬚I⬚NG. But RE⬚A⬚GENT would have played at **15-E** for 84 points. Did you miss any other bingos?

TURN 7.   A A B O O Q T   **SCORE:**   **You**   **Opp**
                                        216   151

1. Do you have a bingo?
2. If no bingo, what should your goal be with this rack?
3. Are there any useful hot spots?
4. Does XI, played earlier at **12-C**, take a front hook?
5. Choose from these plays:

a. BOO(AAQT)	**N-10**	25 points	**d.** BOO(AAQT)	**B-13**	15 points
b. pass seven letters		0 points	**e.** BOA(AOQT)	**N-10**	25 points
c. BOOZED(AAQT)	**N-3**	18 points	**f.** BOAT(AOQ)	**3-L**	19 points

ANSWERS:

1. You have no bingo.
2. If you choose to play as opposed to pass, you should emphasize getting rid of an A and an O. You would need a very good scoring play to justify keeping AA or OO.
3. The TLS at **10-N** looks good. It is next to a vowel so it's worth a hard look.
4. XI does not take a front hook. The only back hook it takes is an S (XIS).
5. The best play is BOA(AOQT) at **N-10** for 25 points. It scores well and breaks up your duplication. A nice double-cross. The B alone produces 18 points.
     Passing is not a real consideration, because 25 points is much too much to give up, especially when you are ahead.
     You should note that the Q without a U is already beginning to cramp your flexibility. Fortunately, you have an A and an O. Keep alert for one of those Q words that doesn't require a U. Do you remember them? Also, with all four U tiles and a blank still unplayed, there is no reason to worry ... yet.
     Your opponent plays SNEE*ZED* at **N-2** for 34 points. A good find.

A C O P Q T T

Opponent's last play—
SNEE*ZED* at **N-2**
34 points

SCORE:	You	Opp
	241	185

DIAGRAM 103

YOUR 8TH TURN

GAME 1
END OF TURN 8

A D I P Q S T

Opponent's last play—
PROD at **M-12**
19 points

SCORE:	You	Opp
	269	204

DIAGRAM 104

YOUR 9TH TURN

TURN 8. A C O P Q T T **SCORE:** You Opp

                                              241   185

1. Do you have a bingo?
2. If no bingo, what should your goals be with this rack?
3. Are there any useful hot spots?
4. What front hooks does TA take (at **10-C**)?
5. Can you find a play at **O-1**?
6. Choose from these plays:

a. TAP(COQT)	**M-12**	13 points	**c.** PACT(COQ)	**M-12**	21 points
b. COAT(PTQ)	**M-12**	17 points	**d.** COAT(PTQ)	**O-1**	28 points

ANSWERS:

1. You have no bingo.
2. You want to do a number of things. You want to use a T to break up the duplication even though TT is not a bad pair. As usual, turnover is important because you want to get at the premium letters remaining (two S tiles and the remaining ▢). Additionally, in this situation, you want turnover so as to get your hands on a U. Holding the Q through several turns is definitely a handicap.
3. The TWS at **1-O** has modest potential, as does the DWS at **13-M**. Note that hot spots are relative. A so-so hot spot can improve as the better hot spots get used. Or, a hot spot can decrease in value as better ones are created.
4. TA takes an E and a U (ETA, UTA).
5. Did you find one?
6. The best play is COAT(PTQ) at **O-1** for 28 points. The hard part is finding the play. If you had identified this as a hot spot, you might have found COAT by a process of elimination, i.e., the only letter in your rack that combines with the S is your O (SO). Of the remaining letters, the N combines only with your A (NA). Likewise, the only letter in your rack that combines with the E is T. This gives you OAT at **O-2**, **O-3**, and **O-4**. By fortunate happenstance, your C goes in front of OAT and you have COAT for 28 points. In effect, you worked backward by letting the board dictate your play rather than by looking in your rack.

    Your opponent plays PROD at **M-12** for 19 points.

TURN 9. A D I P Q S T **SCORE:** You Opp

                                              269   204

1. Do you have a bingo?
2. If no bingo, what should your goals be with this rack?
3. Are there any hot spots?
4. Should you pass ADIPQT and keep the S?
5. Is there anything better than PAS(DIQT) at **E-10** for 31 points?
6. What is your opponent's most likely bingo line?

ANSWERS:

1. You have no bingo.
2. Your first goal should be to get rid of the Q. If you can play it, you should unless you have a much better play (see pp. 163–166). If you can't play it, you should:
   a. Look for a high-scoring play
   b. Go for a high-turnover play (looking for a U or a ▢)
   c. Consider passing
3. There are no special hot spots.
4. If you can't get a decent score or at least some turnover, you should consider passing.
5. Yes. Even though it scores only 15 points, QAID(DPST) at **15-J** is the best play. It costs 16 points, but you are rid of the Q. It leaves you with no vowels, but as consonants go, DPST are quite flexible. Hope you draw a couple of vowels—you had better draw at least one!
6. The most likely place for a bingo is **B-4** to **B-10**. A bingo ending in E will hook on to TA(ETA) at **B-10**. In addition, a bingo ending in ER will play at **B-5** to **B-11**.

    Once you get QAID in your vocabulary, you'll be surprised how often it comes to your rescue.

    Your opponent answers with JUDO at **E-5** for 24 points.

GAME 1
END OF TURN 9

| D | I | P | S | T | U | U |

Opponent's last play—
JUDO at **E-5**
24 points

SCORE: You   Opp
         284   228

DIAGRAM 105

YOUR 10TH TURN

GAME 1
END OF TURN 10

| B | D | I | L | O | T | U |

Opponent's last play—
SILTIER at **B-5**
69 points

SCORE: You   Opp
         306   297

DIAGRAM 106

YOUR 11TH TURN

TURN 10.   D I P S T U U   SCORE: You   Opp

                                      284   228

Finally we get a U!

1. Do you have a bingo?
2. If no bingo, what should your goal be with this rack?
3. What is the only two-letter J word?
4. Are there any useful hot spots?
5. Does KA at **G-14** have a front hook?
6. Choose from these plays:

   a. DUTY(IPSU)   **L-1**   10 points   **c.** PIS(DUUT)   **L-10**   22 points
   b. PITY(DSUU)   **L-1**   12 points   **d.** UPS(DITU)   **L-10**   22 points

ANSWERS:

1. You have no bingo.
2. Try to balance the rack. Use at least one U. UU is a very poor holding. You do not want to keep it longer than necessary.
3. JO is the only two-letter J word.
4. The TLS at **6-F** offers a good double-cross except that you don't have an O to hook on to the J. Too bad. TOP at **F-4** would have been worth 30 points.
5. KA takes an O (OKA).
6. The best play is UPS(DITU) at **L-10** for 22 points. It's better than PIS(DUUT) because it keeps better letters. Keeping DUUT is poor because of the duplication.

   Your opponent plays a bingo, SILTIER at **B-5** for 69 points. This cuts your huge lead to a near tie.

   Allowing this was a serious error. This bingo line could have been stopped. Had your last play been UP(DISTU) at **B-10**, SILTIER could not have been played. Finding UP requires that you know UTA (**10-B**) is a word. Knowing UTA (genus of lizard) would have been worth a lot here.

   Blocking the bingo line would have been a good play. When you have a substantial lead, your opponent needs bingos to catch up. Deprive him!*

*Another play overlooked at the time is PIS(DUUT) at **E-10**. This would have scored well, in addition to blocking the bingo.

TURN 11.   B D I L O T U   SCORE: You   Opp

                                      306   297

1. Do you have a bingo?
2. If no bingo, what should your goal be with this rack?
3. Are there any hot spots?
4. Can you use any of them?
5. Choose from these plays:

   a. IT(BDLOU)   **A-8**   14 points   **c.** BLOT(DIU)   **F-3**   21 points
   b. BLOT(DIU)   **C-3**   16 points   **d.** BUILD(OT)   **A-11** 33 points

ANSWERS:

1. You have no bingo. But close. You almost have OUTBUILD.
2. You should try to score well if possible.
3. The entire "A" column offers hot spots. All three TWSs are open.
4. You can probably use the TWS at **15-A**.
5. BUILD(OT) is best. Points, turnover, etc. The main thing is to find it. If you noticed, RAN would take a B for BRAN. It would be easy to find BUILD.

   Your opponent plays OU[N]CE at **A-1** for 29 points. Normally, you would want more for a blank. At this stage of the game, however, a bingo is unlikely. Also, with the Q played, it is not as necessary to keep the □.

| G | L | O | O | T | | |

Opponent's last play—
OUNCE at **A-1**
29 points

SCORE: You   Opp
           339   326

DIAGRAM 107

YOUR 12TH TURN

| L | O | | | | | |

Opponent's last play—
IT at **8-A**
6 points

SCORE: You   Opp
           358   332

DIAGRAM 108

YOUR 13TH TURN

TURN 12. G L O O T   SCORE:

	You	Opp
	339	326

When your opponent played OUNCE, he picked up the remaining letters. He has two tiles to your five. Unless you are keeping track of the letters played, you won't have any idea what they are. One thing you should do now, if you haven't already, is to check to see if he has a ☐, S, J, K, Q, X, or Z left. As you gain experience, you will learn to keep a running awareness of these letters. For now, it is sufficient to note that all of these key letters have been played.

1. Is there any way you can use all your letters and go out?
2. If you can go out, would it be a good play to take a higher-scoring play that does not go out?
3. If you can't go out, what should your goals be with this rack?
4. Are there any useful hot spots?
5. Does WE at **F-14** take a front hook?
6. Choose from these plays:

a. GOT(LO)	**F-4**	19 points		**c.** GLO*W*(OT)	**2-G**	8 points
b. LOOT(G)	**F-3**	19 points		**d.** GOOP(LT)	**11-I**	14 points

ANSWERS:

1. You can't go out on this turn.
2. Perhaps. Remember, if you go out, you get two times the value of your opponent's remaining letters. If you postpone going out, and your opponent goes out himself, he gets the bonus. By waiting, you lose:
   a. The bonus you would have received
   b. The bonus your opponent gets for going out
   c. The value of his final turn. Remember, if you go out, your opponent gets no more turns.
   As a rule, you should always go out unless you know your opponent can't, i.e., usually when he has an unplayable Q.
3. Since you can't go out in one turn, you should try to ensure going out in two turns if possible. Also, you should try to use your big letters immediately so as to minimize the penalty if your opponent goes out first.
4. In the end game, when it sometimes is hard to score, hot spots become relative. A place that you would normally ignore can become quite worthwhile.
   In this light, you should look at spots like these. Hypothetically, you might have:

14-L	MOON	16 points	**F-5**	OP	29 points
I-3	ONE	12 points	**C-6**	FA	14 points
13-F	OOH	19 points	**K-6**	HEFT	15 points
K-10	MU	20 points	**K-3**	OVA	21 points

   Actually, some of these are pretty impressive. Simply speaking, you should not lose heart when the board looks cramped.
5. WE takes 3 front hooks: AEO, to form the words AWE, EWE, and OWE.
6. Both GOT(LO) at F-4 and LOOT(G) at F-3 are good plays. They score 5 points more than the next play. GOT was chosen in the actual game.
   Your opponent plays I*T* at **8-A** for 6 points.

TURN 13. L O   SCORE:

	You	Opp
	358	332

You've won the game, and if you play in a light-hearted group, your opponent may already be bagging the tiles for another game. If you are of a mind to finish the game and get a few more bragging points, you can look for the best play. What is it? *Clue:* it's worth 10 points. *Another clue:* there are two 10-point plays.

They are:

a. LO*P*	at **11-J**	10 points
b. *L*OON	at **14-L**	10 points

You choose LOON and go out (diagram 109). This gives you 368 points. Your opponent has an I left, so you get 2 more points to make the final score 370 to 332.

Scrabble Board

	A	B	C	D	E	F	G	H	I	J	K	L	M	N	O
1	O₁														C₃
2	U₁						W₄						S₁	O₁	
3	N₁					H₄							N₁	A₁	
4	C₃		G₂		N₁	A₁	V₄	Y₄				N₁	E₁	T₁	
5	E₁	S₁	J₈	O₁		L₁						E₁			
6		I₁	U₁	T₁		E₁				Z₁₀					
7		L₁	D₂	H₄	A₁	R₁	E₁	M₃		E₁					
8	I₁	T₁	M₃	O₄	V₄	I₁	E₁		F₄	E₁	N₁	D₂	S₁		
9	I₁		O₁		F₄	R₁	Y₄						T₁		
10		E₁	T₁	A₁					U₁		B₃	E₁			
11	B₃	R₁	A₁	N₁					P₃		O₁	E₁			
12	U₁	X₈	I₁					S₁	P₃	A₁	R₁				
13	I₁		N₁						R₁		I₁				
14	L₁		G₂	A₁	W₄	K₅			L₁	O₁	O₁	N₁			
15	D₂		T₁	E₁	A₁	R₁	Q₁₀	A₁	I₁	D₂		G₂			

FINAL BOARD

DIAGRAM 109

SCORE:

You	Opp
368	
+ 2	
370	332

Very respectable.

There are a few observations worth making here:

1. Neither player had exceptional letters, yet the final score topped 700 points in total.
2. Both players had a blank. The final margin was probably due to the fact that your blank came at a more opportune time. A little slice of luck.
3. Both players had two big letters. You got good mileage from the Z, but not much from the Q. At least it was a painless Q.

   Your opponent got excellent value from the X, and moderate value from the J.
4. None of the words used in this game were unusual, with the possible exception of some two-letter words. Some people feel they need to know unusual words to do well, but that just isn't true. Unusual words *do* help, but the important talent is finding the word you already know.
5. Especially, you should note how important those two-letter words were. Without them, there would have been no:
   - **a.** TAXI(**C-10**)   39 points (TA, AN, XI, IN)
   - **b.** OUNCE(**A-1**)   29 points (ES)
   - **c.** FRY(**9-G**)   28 points (ER, IF)
   - **d.** TEAR(**15-E**)   25 points (AT, WE, KA)
   - **e.** BOA(**N-10**)   25 points (BE, DE, AR)
   - **f.** FENDS(**8-K**)   40 points (EF, ME)
   - **g.** COAT(**O-1**)   28 points (SO, NA, ET)
   - **h.** GOT(**F-4**)   19 points (JO, UT)
6. Note the hooks:
   - **a.** AR at **12-N** was turned into PAR and then SPAR
   - **b.** AN at **11-D** was turned into RAN and then BRAN
   - **c.** ZED at **N-6** was turned into SNEEZED
7. Post mortems: On turn 5, ZED(ENRT☐) was played at **N-6** for 33 points. Later on, two better plays were pointed out by kibitzers.

   REZONE☒(T) at **E-5** was worth 69 points and INTERZONE, a bingo, at **13-C** was worth 68.

   On turn 6, BOAT(AOQ) at **N-10** tallied 27 points and had better turnover.

GAME 2

Match your skills against two top tournament players.

TURN 1.   A F G I O R T

1. Do you have a bingo?
2. If no bingo, what should your goals be with this rack?
3. Consider your play.
4. Choose from these plays:

a.	TRIG(AFO)	**8-F**	10 points	**c.**	FROG(AIT)	**8-F**	16 points
b.	GRAFT(IO)	**8-D**	22 points	**d.**	FAGOT(IR)	**8-D**	26 points

ANSWERS:

1. You have no bingo.
2. Your goals should be:
   a. To put the F or G on the DLS
   b. To use as many letters as possible (turnover)
   c. To keep as flexible letters as possible
3. What plays did you find?
4. FAGOT(IR) at **8-D** for 26 points is best. FAGOT exposes a DLS but since playing safe (at **8-E**) would cost 8 points, it isn't worth it.

   Note that you could play GRAFT(IO) at **8-D** for 22 points and expose no DLSs. The safety makes GRAFT worth considering. The reason you don't play it is that GRAFT leaves you with (IO). FAGOT leaves you with the much better (IR).

   FROG and TRIG suffer from fewer points and lesser turnover.

   Your opponent plays ABACA at **E-8** for 18 points.

*Turn 1. The best play was one not considered during the game. FORGAT(I) at **8-D** was worth 28 points.

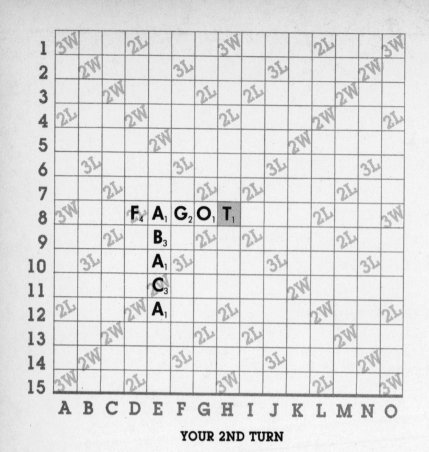

| A | E | E | I | M | P | R |

Opponent's last play—
ABACA at **E-8**
18 points

SCORE:	You	Opp
	26	18

DIAGRAM 110

YOUR 2ND TURN

| A | E | E | I | O | P | R |

Opponent's last play—
pass seven

SCORE:	You	Opp
	52	18

DIAGRAM 111

YOUR 3RD TURN

TURN 2.   A E E I M P R   SCORE: You   Opp

                                    26   18

1. Do you have a bingo?
2. If no bingo, what should your goals be with this rack?
3. Are there any useful hot spots?
4. Consider your play.
5. Choose from these plays:
   a. GEM(AEIPR)   **F-8**   26 points   **d.** PRAM(EEI)   **D-12**   30 points
   b. ME(AEIPR)   **D-12**   16 points   **e.** IMAGE(EPR)   **F-5**   18 points
   c. MAP(EEIR)   **9-G**   22 points

ANSWERS:

1. You have no bingo. But very, very close. You have excellent letters.
2. Your goals should be:
   a. To score well
   b. But not to ruin the good quality of your rack
3. The hot spots are:
   a. The DWS at **12-D**   **d.** The DLSs at **7-G** and **7-I**
   b. The TLS at **10-F**   **e.** The DWS at **13-C** if you could hook on to ABACA
   c. The DLSs at **9-G** and **9-I**
4. What plays did you find?
5. Your best play is GEM(AEIPR) at **F-8** for 26 points. It keeps excellent letters, uses one of your duplicated E tiles, and is safe. PRAM(EEI) at **D-12** would score 4 more points, but it would keep poor letters, plus it would open up the TWSs at **15-A** and **15-M**. The gain is not worth the risk.
   Your opponent passes all seven letters.

TURN 3.   A E E I O P R   SCORE: You   Opp

                                    52   18

1. Do you have a bingo?
2. If not, what should your goals be with this rack?
3. Are there any useful hot spots?
4. Can you put a single letter in front of C at **11-E**?
5. What hook does AM (**10-E**) take?
6. Consider your play.
7. Choose from these plays:
   a. OPERATE(I)   **H-3**   12 points   **d.** PA(EEIOR)   **D-12**   16 points
   b. Pass seven letters   0 points   **e.** PORE(AEI)   **D-12**   22 points
   c. OPERA(EI)   **9-H**   12 points

ANSWERS:

1. You have no bingo. The last draw (EO) was not good.
2. Your goals should be:
   a. To break up the AO combination
   b. To get as much turnover as possible
3. There are not as many hot spots as on the previous turn. Still open are the DWSs at **12-D** and **13-C**. Also, the DLSs at **7-G** and **7-I**.
4. C, Q, V, and Z do not make two-letter words.
5. AM takes an A, I, P, or U: AMA, AMI, AMP, AMU.
6. What did you find?
7. The best play is OPERATE at **H-3** for 12 points. You don't have a good dump play and the higher-scoring plays have serious faults. PA(EEIOR) at **D-12** for 16 points keeps too many vowels.
   PORE(ATE) at **D-12** for 22 points keeps fine letters but opens up the entire 15 row. You need to improve your score by at least 15 points to justify giving direct shots at TWSs.
   Much better is to take the 12 points plus the hidden value of turnover.
   Your opponent plays SURROUND at **3-D** for 61 points. A fine example of using the board. His rack was an unpromising DNRRSUU and yet he came up with a bingo. Very good play. I imagine your opponent is quite pleased with himself.

I I I L L N ☐

Opponent's last play—
SURROUND at **3-D**
61 points

SCORE: You   Opp
             64   79

DIAGRAM 112

YOUR 4TH TURN

TURN 4.   I I I L L N ☐   SCORE: You   Opp

                          64   79

1. Do you have a bingo?
2. If no bingo, what should your goal be with this rack?
3. Are there any useful hot spots?
4. Which of these are real words that could hook on to the E at **9-H**? ED, EF, EH, EL, EM, EN, EP, ER, ES, ET, EW, EX, and EY.
5. What would you do?
6. Choose from these plays:

    a. NAIL(IIL☐)   **7-G**   9 points   **d.** Pass one (IILLN☐)   0 points
    b. *LAIN*(IIL☐)   **12-D**   14 points   **e.** *DILL*(IIN☐)   **K-3**   10 points
    c. Pass six (☐)   0 points   **f.** ILL(IIN☐)   **G-10**   8 points

ANSWERS:

1. You have no bingo.
2. You want either to score or to achieve a better-balanced rack.
3. There are some good places to play here:
    a. An H at **4-D**
    b. The DLSs at **7-G**, **7-I**, and **9-I**
    c. The DWS at **12-D**
4. ED, EP, EW, and EY are phonies. The rest are real.
5. What was your choice?
6. NAIL(IIL☐) and LAIN(IIL☐) both score poorly and they keep duplicated I tiles.

    Passing one I and keeping (IILLN☐) is poor because if you miss, you are no better off than before. You have a 32 percent chance of drawing a bingo but many of them won't be playable.

    DILL(IIN☐) at **K-3** for 10 points is just marginally acceptable because your leave (IIN☐) is decent. The double I tiles are not as bad as normal because you have an N, which can be used in an ING or ION ending. One bad thing about DILL at **K-3** is that it blocks some of your bingo rows.

    ILL(IIN☐), even though it scores only 8 points, is reasonable because it gets rid of some duplication and does not block any potential bingo lines as did DILL. The best play is not clearcut. The one actually chosen was to pass six, keeping the blank.

    Your opponent plays FOCI at **4-A** for 30 points.

    This is dangerous but probably justified since he is scoring quite well.

| A | A | E | E | T | Y | □ |

Opponent's last play—
FOCI at **4-A**
30 points

SCORE:	You	Opp
	64	109

DIAGRAM 113

YOUR 5TH TURN

TURN 5. A A E E T Y □   SCORE: You   Opp

                                    64   109

1. Do you have a bingo?
2. If no bingo, what should your goals be with this rack?
3. Are there any useful hot spots?
4. What front hook does OPERATE at **H-3** take?
5. Does SI (**D-3**) take a front hook?
6. Do you see anything good?
7. Choose from these plays:
    a. YEA(AET□)   **D-12**   22 points
    b. AYE(AET□)   **4-K**   15 points
    c. FAT⊤Y(AEE)   **A-4**   30 points

ANSWERS:

1. You have no bingo.
2. Your goal is to get rid of your duplication and the Y if possible. If it seems to you that you have this same general goal turn after turn, it's true your basic Scrabble® play is to combine scoring with rack balance and is the case here. If you can play off the AEY, you will be left with (AET□). Remember that the best group of letters to draw to is the AERST (RATES) group. (AET□) qualifies perfectly.
3. The "A" column looks very good.
4. COOPERATE. When your opponent played FOCI on his last turn, he could have played COOPERATE (39 points) instead. He probably overlooked it.
5. SI takes a P: PSI
6. What did you do?
7. Your best play is YEA(AET□) at **D-12** for 22 points. It scores well, and it uses exactly the letters you wish to use. It does open up the 15 row, but your opponent needs specific letters to do that.
    What letters hook on to YEA? H, N, R, and S for YEAH, YEAN (to bear young), YEAR, and YEAS.
    AYE(AET□) at **4-K** for 15 points is safe, but it scores 7 fewer points. Note that if your opponent can't use this spot, you probably can since you have the □.
    FAT⊤Y(EE) at **A-4** for 30 points is terrible. You need much better mileage from your □. Your opponent plays FOOLING at **A-4** for 33 points.

A	E	E	E	P	T	□

Opponent's last play—
FOOLING at **A-4**
33 points

SCORE:	You	Opp
	86	142

DIAGRAM 114

YOUR 6TH TURN

TURN 6.   A E E E P T □   SCORE: You   Opp

                                     86   142

1. Do you have a bingo?
2. If you have no bingo, what should your goals be with this rack?
3. Are there any useful hot spots?
4. Does YA at **12-D** take a front hook?
5. What play do you like?
6. Choose from these plays:
   a. PAT(EEE□)   **B-6**   25 points
   b. PEE(AET□)   **5-D**   15 points

ANSWERS:
1. Yes, you have a bingo: *R*EPEATE□ at **6-H** for 67 points.*
2. If you didn't find the bingo, you would want to balance your rack by playing two or three vowels.
3. The TLS at **6-B** looks good.
4. YA takes a P or an R in front; PYA or RYA.
5. Did you find the bingo?
6. Play *R*EPEATED. Note that in spite of three E tiles, you had a common bingo. Triple E tiles are not automatically bad. They may look silly on your rack, but in practice they can be productive.

   If you had to choose between PAT and PEE, it would be closer than the 10-point difference would suggest. PAT(EEE□) at **B-6** scores 25, but it keeps three E tiles. Not terrible, as already noted, but certainly nowhere nearly as good as (AET□), which is your leave when you play PEE(AET□) at **5-D**.

   Your opponent plays XI at **B-6** for 52. Hard to keep up with him. You get a bingo and he answers with a two-letter play that scores almost as well. That X is a powerful tile!

* [R]EPA*R*TEE at **6-D** would have been a safer bingo.

	A	B	C	D	E	F	G	H	I	J	K	L	M	N	O
1	3W			2L				3W				2L			3W
2		2W				3L				3L				2W	
3			2W	S	U	R	R	O	U	N	D		2W		
4	F	O	C	I				P				2W			2L
5	O				2W			E			2W				
6	O	X				3L		R	E	P	E	A	T	E	D
7	L	I	2L				2L	A	2L				2L		
8	I			F	A	G	O	T				2L			3W
9	N		2L		B	E	2L	E	2L				2L		
10	G	3L			A	M				3L				3L	
11					C						2W				
12	2L			Y	A			2L				2W			2L
13			2W	E			2L		2L				2W		
14		2W		A		3L				3L				2W	
15	3W			2L				3W				2L			3W

YOUR 7TH TURN

GAME 2
END OF TURN 6

A	D	E	Q	U	Y	Z

Opponent's last play—
XI at **B-6**
52 points

SCORE:	**You**	**Opp**
	153	**194**

DIAGRAM 115

TURN 7. A D E Q U Y Z SCORE: You   Opp
                                     153   194

1. Do you have a bingo?
2. If no bingo, what should your goals be with this rack?
3. Are there any useful hot spots?
4. Does OX at **6-A** take a back hook?
5. Does XI at **B-6** take a back hook?
6. Do you see a good play? There is a nonbingo play worth 70 points available.
7. Choose from these plays:

a.	QUA(ADEYZ)	**14-B**	24 points	e.	QUAY(ADEZ)	**L-4**	32 points
b.	QUA(ADEYZ)	**L-4**	24 points	f.	DAZE(QUY)	**10-H**	45 points
c.	QU*O*(ADEYZ)	**B-2**	24 points	g.	*DAZED*(QUY)	**O-6**	42 points
d.	QUAY(ADEZ)	**14-B**	32 points				

8. Does QUA take a front hook?

ANSWERS:

1. You have no bingo.
2. Your goals should be:
   a. To use the Q
   b. To get a big score. Lots of good places to play here.
3. Hot spots are the DWS at **5-K**, the "O" column, and the DWS at **14-B** in conjunction with the TLS at **14-F**.
4. OX takes Y: OXY.
5. XI takes an S: XIS.
6. QUEAZY(AD) at **14-A** for 70 points.
7. QUEAZY is obviously best. It scores more than your previous bingo did, it gets rid of the Q, it achieves turnover, and it is reasonably safe.

   Of the other plays, QUO is a phony. No good.

   If you choose between DAZE (**H-10**) and *DAZED* (**O-6**), you should play DAZE(QUY) at **H-10** for 45 points. This leaves the "O" column and the 15 row open so you will have a sure shot at a TWS. If you played *DAZED*(QUY) at **O-6**, your opponent might grab the 15 row for a good score. You would have no really fine spot to play. Remember, try to leave an even number of hot spots.
8. QUA takes an A in front, AQUA. Be aware that a play such as QUA at **14-B** is not too safe. Your opponent could play (hypothetically) WEAK (**A-12**) for 58 points.

   Your opponent plays B*E*HOWL at **5-G** for 49 points. An amazing play. It includes four hooks plus the word itself is hard to find. A really fine play.

A D L L R T V

Opponent's last play—
BEHOWL at **5-G**
49 points

SCORE: You   Opp
         223   243

DIAGRAM 116

YOUR 8TH TURN

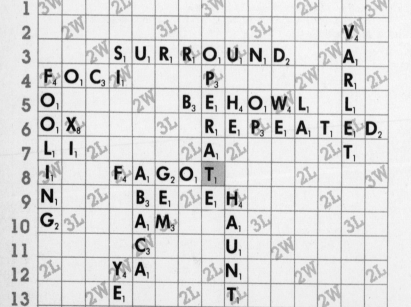

D I I L O S T

Opponent's last play—
HAUNTED at **I-9**
75 points

SCORE: You   Opp
         241   318

DIAGRAM 117

YOUR 9TH TURN

TURN 8.   A D L L R T V   SCORE: You   Opp

                                          223   243

1. Do you have a bingo?
2. If no bingo, what should your goal be with this rack?
3. Are there any useful hot spots?
4. What are the two-letter words beginning with Y?
5. Can you find a decent play?
6. Choose from these plays:
   a. *DART*(DLLV)   **O-6**   9 points   **d.** VAR*LET*(DL)   **N-2**   18 points
   b. ART(DLLV)   **15-F**   14 points   **e.** Pass all seven letters   0 points
   c. R*EV*(ADLLT)   **C-13**   16 points

ANSWERS:

1. You have no bingo.
2. To play off as many letters as possible.
3. The 15 row, the "O" column, and the DLSs at **7-G** and **7-I**.
4. Y takes an A and an E: YA and YE.
5. It wasn't easy.
6. VAR*LET*(DL) at **N-2** for 18 points is the only reasonable play. The other plays score poorly and they keep horrid letters. Better to pass seven letters than to make a play that keeps bad letters plus gets no score. One or the other maybe, but not both. VAR*LET* is much superior to passing because you get fair points and a fair leave (DL).
     Your opponent plays HAUNTED at **I-9** for 75 points. This may be hard to overcome.

TURN 9.   D I I L O S T   SCORE: You   Opp

                                          241   318

1. Do you have a bingo?
2. If no bingo, what should your goals be with this rack?
3. Are there any useful hot spots?
4. If you hope to use the "O" column (**O-6**), you will have to hook on to the T at **7-N**. What are the two-letter T words?
5. Do you have a good play?
6. Choose from these plays:
   a. LIST(DIO)   **8-L**   25 points   **d.** *DILDO*(IST)   **O-6**   17 points
   b. LI*DO*(DIST)   **15-G**   15 points   **e.** IDIOT(DLS)   **15-H**   21 points
   c. DI*D*(IOLST)   **15-G**   15 points

ANSWERS:

1. You have no bingo.
2. Your goals are:
   a. Turnover
   b. To create bingo lines. You trail by 77 points, so you will need a bingo to get back in the game.
3. Hot spots are the 15 row.
4. T takes A, I, and O: TA, TI, and TO.
5. Nothing really good here.
6. IDIOT(DLS) at **15-H** for 21 points is best. LI*DO*(DIST) at **15-G** for 15 points is a so-so, second best. IDIOT is better because it scores 6 extra points plus it turns over one extra letter. IDIOT opens two useful bingo columns (L and M) and uses the hot spot in the 15 row. LI*DO* gives you the "K" column if you have a bingo ending in S. IDIOT, therefore, leaves more bingo chances than LI*DO* and is therefore a better play.
     LIST(DIO) at **8-L** for 25 points is a bad play because it uses your important S.
     Your opponent plays D̄IMER at **O-6** for 20 points. Curious word. It means a molecule made of two like molecules.

GAME 2
END OF TURN 9

D	E	I	L	S	T	W

Opponent's last play—
DIMER at **O-6**
20 points

SCORE:	**You**	**Opp**
	262	**338**

YOUR 10TH TURN

DIAGRAM 118

TURN 10. D E I L S T W   SCORE: You   Opp
                                          262   338

Considering our score, we are in a lot of trouble. Usually, at this stage, 262 is good for a decent lead.

1. Do you have a bingo?
2. Where can you play it if you have one?
3. If no bingo, what should your goals be with this rack?
4. Are there any new useful hot spots?
5. What two-letter words end in R? Can you play in the "N" column at **N-9** or **N-10**?
6. What is your play?
7. Choose from these plays:

   a. *W*ED(EILST) **C-13** 24 points   **c.** WELD(ITS) **N-9** 19 points
   b. *N*EWT(DILS) **12-I** 14 points   **d.** *W*ASTED(IL) **7-G** 46 points

ANSWERS:

1. You have a bingo, WILDEST, but you can't play it.
2. Places you might have been able to play a bingo are:
   a. A nine-letter bingo at **K-5**
   b. A nine-letter bingo at **L-5**
   c. An eight-letter bingo at **11-G** or **11-H**
   d. An eight-letter bingo at **12-G** or **12-H**
   e. An eight-letter bingo at **13-G** or **13-H**
   f. An eight-letter bingo at **14-H** (very unlikely)
   g. An eight-letter bingo at **K-8**
   h. An eight-letter bingo at **L-8**
   i. A seven-letter bingo at **N-9** (requires two-letter hooks with the E at **O-9** and the R at **O-10**)
3. Goals are:
   a. Not to block bingo lines
   b. To score
   c. To improve your rack balance
4. No useful hot spots.
5. Two-letter words ending in R are AR, ER, OR. If IR were acceptable, WILDEST would fit at **N-9**. Too bad.
6. Did you see WASTED?
7. The best play is pretty clearly *W*ASTED(IL) at **7-G**. It scores very well, and, importantly, it doesn't block your prime bingo lines.

   Of the other three possible plays in diagram 118 (not shown), *W*ED is better than the other two. *W*ED (**C-13**) scores 24 points but this is not the main reason it is better than *N*EWT (**12-I**) or WELD (**N-9**). Both *N*EWT and WELD destroy bingo lines when your main concern should be to save, or even to increase, your bingo lines. Look at diagram 118 and see the effect *N*EWT and WELD would have on the bingo lines outlined in answer 2, above.

   Note the placement of *W*ASTED (**7-G**). It includes five hooks, one two-letter word (WO), and four three-letter words (HES, OPT, WEE, and LAD). This is most unusual. Multiple hooks are usually made up of two-letter words. Scoring four three-letter words is exceptional.

   Finding a play like this is difficult, but not as difficult as the original awareness that such plays exist. When you realize that multiple hooks can be found and start to look for them, they will become moderately common.

   Your opponent plays JOINERS at **M-9** for 99 points!

   That's probably the old ball game. It would have been easy to block this but that wasn't in your interest. This way, you lose the game by a lot. Had you blocked the bingo lines, you would have lost by less, but a loss nonetheless. When you are behind, you have to take some risks. Sometimes it works, sometimes it doesn't. Here, it didn't.

A D G I L N N

Opponent's last play—
JOINERS at **M-9**
99 points

SCORE:	You	Opp
	308	437

DIAGRAM 119

YOUR 11TH TURN

A I N L

Opponent's last play—
VINO at **12-K**
14 points

SCORE:	You	Opp
	327	451

DIAGRAM 120

YOUR 12TH TURN

TURN 11. A D G I L N N **SCORE:** You 308   Opp 437

Trailing by 129, it's going to be difficult to win this game. JOINERS not only gave your opponent a huge bingo, it blocked almost all of your bingo spots. To make matters worse, if possible, your opponent puts the bag down and announces that there are only 5 tiles left. You have to score 130 points on this turn, counting penalty points.

1. Do you have a bingo?
2. If not, or if you have a bingo and can't play it, what should your goal be with this rack?
3. Can you play a letter at **9-N** to make a J—E word?
4. Can you play a letter at **10-N** to make an O—R word?
5. Given different letters in your rack, could you make a word at **N-9**?
6. Choose from these plays:
     a. DANG(AILN)   **10-H**   19 points
     b. GIRD(ALNN)   **4-L**   28 points
     c. GLAD(INN)   **L-10**   24 points

ANSWERS:

1. For the second consecutive turn, you have an unplayable bingo: LANDING. Unlucky. Actually, even if it were playable, the game couldn't be won. JOINERS was too much to overcome.
2. Your goal should be to take what points you can get and to go out in two plays.
3. Yes, you can make JEE and JOE.
4. Yes, you can make OAR and OUR.
5. Yes, a number of them. OAF at **N-9** would be worth 28 points.
6. GIRD(ALNN) at **4-L** for 28 points is best. In practice, this play was overlooked, and the lesser alternative of DANG(AILN) at **10-H** was selected. Typical of lost games when attention to detail weakens.
       Your opponent plays VINO at **12-K** for 14 points.

TURN 12. A I N L **SCORE:** You 327   Opp 451

Your opponent has two tiles left.
1. Does your opponent have an S, ☐, J, Q, X, or Z?
2. Can you use all four of your letters?

ANSWERS:

1. Your opponent has two of the premium letters, an S and a K.
2. Yes, you can play NAIL at **2-I** for 15 points (see diagram 121).

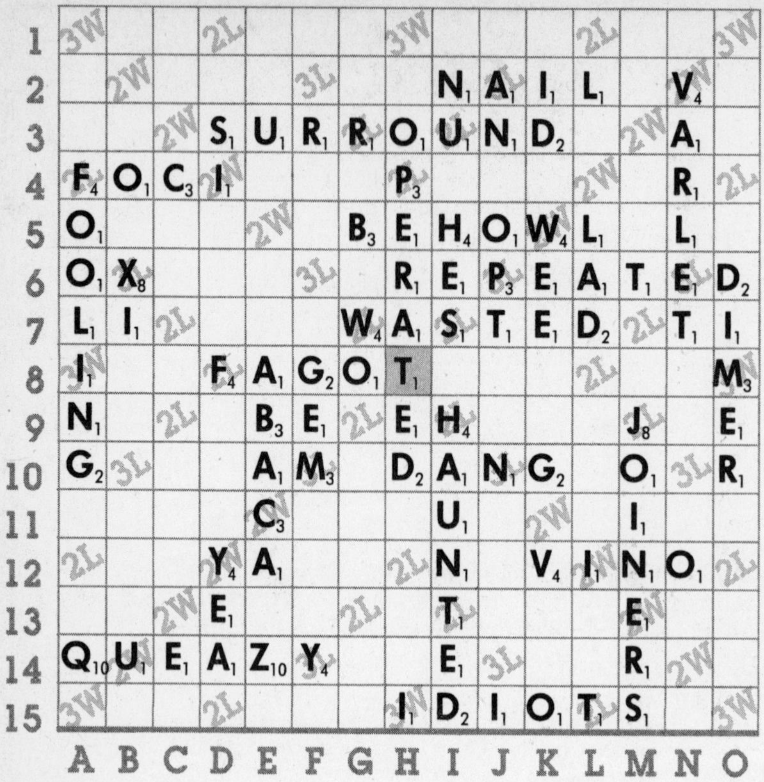

FINAL BOARD

GAME 2
END OF TURN 12
COMPLETED GAME

SCORE:	You	Opp
	342	
	+12	
	354	451

DIAGRAM 121

Final Score:

Counting the 12-point penalty from your opponent's K and S:

You	Opp
342	
+ 12	
354	451

A decent score to lose with. Amazing to score 354 points and not be in contention.

In fact, it was a fairly close game until the end. You had two unplayable bingos, which didn't help. Had you been able to play either of your bingos and also to block your opponent's JOINERS, it would have been a swing of about 180 points. Enough to win the game.

FOR THE CURIOUS

This section is intended to cover a few odds and ends that are pertinent to Scrabble®, but not quite suitable for the earlier sections. "For the Curious" is a combination of odd-word lists plus some pointers on how to improve your game.

Covered here are:

1. A list of phony words

2. A list of real, but odd-looking, words

3. A list of three-letter words that can be made by adding a single letter to a two-letter word. This is called the Two-to-Make-Three List.

4. A list of the most common seven-letter words

5. A list of the most common eight-letter words

6. A list of ten specific six-letter groups that are the basis for many bingos

7. Some suggestions on how to improve your game

8. A list of current useful publications and Scrabble® clubs

PHONY WORDS

A

ADE	AIRBAG	ANTSY	AXER	BANDITO
ADONIS	AIREDALE	ARTESIAN	AZTEC	BANQUE
AEROBICS	AIRFARE	ARTSY		BETTIE
AFRO	AJAX	ATLANTIC	**B**	BETTY
AFTS	ALOT	ATOW		BICEP
AGEIST	AMIC	AUTOMAT	BACKDATE	BINGED
AHS	ANNUM	AVIS	BALDY	BINGOES
AINT	ANOREXIC	AWER	BAM	BIOTECH
			BANDAID	

BIRDY
BIZ
BON
BONAFIDE
BONK
BOWIE
BOWTIE
BRAZO
BRITE
BROAST
BRIQUET
BUILTIN
BURNUP
BURRITO

C

CABBED
CABLER
CAGER
CAJUN
CAKY
CALIMARI
CANOER
CAPLET
CARPOOL
CHABLIS
CHINUP
CHIVED
CLUNKY
COEDIT
COILY
COLBY
COMP
CONDO
CORNISH
CORONATE
COVENT
COVERUP
CRAZIES
CUER
CURATED
CURVABLE

D

DANE
DANISH
DATABASE
DEADBOLT
DELITE

DERUST
DESKTOP
DETOX
DEVINE
DEXY
DINERY
DIXIE
DINTY
DISKETTE
DOBERMAN
DOGTAG
DOLBY
DORK
DOWNSIDE
DULCE
DUTCHED

E

EARLIKE
EDAM
EDEN
EEK
EELER
EGGY
ELECTEE
ELFS
ENDGAME
ENDZONE
ESKIMO
ETON
EXED
EXING
EXEUNT

F

FAB
FACELIFT
FADEOUT
FAIRE
FAKEOUT
FANGY
FEEDINGS
FEM
FEST
FEVERY
FIBIA
FIGGY
FILMER
FLIM

FLOSSED
FOLIC
FOOLER
FORMICA
FREON
FREEBASE
FRITZ
FUDGY
FUNGOS
FUNSTER
FUTON
FUTZ
FUTZED

G

GAITERED
GAMESMAN
GATESMAN
GELATO
GENTRIFY
GIDDUP
GIRDERED
GLITZ
GLITZY
GOATY
GOCART
GOLIATH
GOOPY
GOUDA
GOV
GRAHAMS
GRANOLA
GRIDLOCK
GROK
GROTTY
GROUPY
GRUYERE
GULA
GUNKY

H

HAIKUS
HASBEEN
HAIRNET
HALFED
HALFS
HARAKIRI
HEADLIKE
HEE

HEMAN
HERBED
HIGHRISE
HOFBRAU
HOTLINE
HYPED
HYPER

I

IBID
ICER
IDE
IDEE
ILLEGALS
IMAGER
IMPROV
INARTFUL
INCA
INDIAN
INFIGHT
INKILY
INKSPOT
INLAW
INSUREE
IRONAGE
ITER

J

JA
JADY
JELLO
JESTILY
JETLAG
JINGOS
JIVER
JOKEY
JOS
JOVE
JUPITER
JURIED

K

KELLY
KEYER
KEWPIE
KIEV
KIR
KLEIG

KLEENEX
KNIVE

L

LAPTOP
LATIN
LEANERS
LEVIS
LILLY
LINOTYPE
LIPREAD
LITE
LORDY
LUCITE
LUKE
LUNARY
LYCRA

M

MAYO
MED
MEGABYTE
MELBA
MELTDOWN
MENS
MIDCALF
MIDEAST
MIDLIFE
MIDWEST
MIDWING
MIN
MINDSET
MING
MINORLY
MISALIGN
MIT
MOANER
MOHAWK
MOONWALK
MOUNTIE
MOUNTY
MUNCHY
MUNK
MURIC

N

NACHO
NEOLITE

NEPTUNE
NERD
NEWSTEAM
NINJA
NITCH
NITE
NITERY
NOHS
NON
NONGAY
NORDIC
NOSECONE
NUKED
NURD
NUTSY
NYET

O

OFFCOLOR
OFFSIDES
OLYMPIC
ONER
ONLOAD
ONLINE
ONLOOK
ONSIDES
OUI
OUIJA
OUTLEAD
OUTLIED
OUTRAIN
OUTRISE
OUTSAY
OVERLIT
OVERNITE
OVERTIP
OWER

P

PAGER
PAIRINGS
PAYLESS
PERMED
PESTO
PESTY
PICANTE
PICO
PINEDROP
PINER

PIXEL
PLACINGS
PLUTO
POGO
POLKADOT
POM
PONG
PONT
PRE
PRELAW
PRETRIAL
PROMO
PROXIED
PSYCHED
PYREX

Q

QAT
QUO
QUONSET
QUORA
QUICKY

R

RA
RAGDOLL
RANDIER
RANKINGS
RAUNCH
REALINE
REALTOR
REBAKE
REDEAL
REDIALS
REDLINE
REGALISM
REGGAE
REINK
RELAYER
REPARENT
REPLOW
REPO
REPOT
REQUOTE
RESTAIN
RETAPE
RETAX
RETILE
REUBEN

RICY
RICEY
RINGY
RIPOFF
ROADIES
ROADSIGN
ROM
ROMEO
ROSEHIPS
ROYALE
RUMPOT
RUTIN

S

SAGGY
SARAN
SCOWER
SCOPED
SCOPING
SEABEE
SEAGULL
SEALION
SEATBELT
SHACKED
SHOEBOX
SHOOTIST
SITCOM
SITUP
SITZ
SIXER
SLAMMER
SLANTER
SLEAZE
SOFABED
SPACY
SPAM
SPARTAN
SPRITZ
SQUIRTY
STUNTMAN
SUSHI

T

TAILFIN
TAKEUP
TEABAG
TECH
TEFLON

TEMP
TET
TIERACK
TIMELINE
TIMEZONE
TIX
TOCK
TOKED
TOMATOS
TONITE
TOSTADA
TOUGHED
TOXICS
TRICEP
TROJAN
TUNEUP
TWILITE
TWINK
TWINKY
TWISTY

U

UFO
UNBUSY
UNEROTIC
UNJAM
UNLIKED
UNNEAT
UNRISKY
UNTILED
UPRATES
UPRISED
UPSCALE

V

VASELINE
VEGGY
VELCRO
VENUS
VIBE
VICTROLA
VIG
VIP
VIRGO
VISUALS
VULCAN

W

WAM
WANG
WARHORSE
WARPAINT
WIMP
WIMPY
WINLESS
WINTERIZE
WISEGUY
WISEMAN
WISK
WORDLIST
WOWIE

X

XRAY

Y

YANKEE
YIKES
YING
YO
YOYO
YUCK
YUCKY
YUM
YUPPIE

Z

ZEN
ZESTILY
ZINGERS
ZINK
ZIT
ZOAS
ZONK
ZOOT
ZORIS
ZULU

Strange-Looking Real Words

A

ABETTER	One who abets
ADDAX	A large antelope
ADIOS	Farewell
ADMAN	Someone in the advertising business
AGA	A Turkish officer
ALAMO	A softwood tree
ALAN	A hunting dog
ALASKA	A type of heavy fabric
ALLHEAL	A medicinal herb
ALOHA	A Hawaiian greeting
ALWAY	Always
AMIGA	A female friend
APELIKE	Like an ape
ARCO	An instruction to players of stringed instruments
AVGAS	Jet fuel

B

BAGWIG	An eighteenth-century wig
BAHT	A monetary unit of Thailand
BANGKOK	A straw hat
BAREFIT	Barefoot
BATMAN	An assistant
BIJOU	A jewel
BOFFO	A hearty laugh
BONEYARD	A junkyard
BROCOLI	A variant spelling of *broccoli*
BUZZWORD	A technical phrase

C

CALIF	A Muslim leader
CAMELEER	A camel driver
CIAO	An expression of greeting or farewell
CISCO	A freshwater fish
CIVVY	A civilian
COMMY	A Communist
COWPAT	A dropping of cow dung
CUPPA	A cup of tea
CYDER	Cider

D

DENAZIFY	To rid of Nazis
DHAK	An Asian tree
DINERO	A coin of Peru
DOGDOM	The world of dogs
DRAFFY	Worthless
DUMKY	A Slavic folk ballad
DUSTUP	An argument

E

EARTHPEA	A twining plant
EPIZOOTY	A type of animal disease
ERUCT	To belch
EXEC	An executive officer
EXURBIA	The residential area beyond the suburbs
EYESHOT	The range of an individual's vision

F

FANDOM	A group of admirers
FERBAM	A fungicide
FIGEATER	A large beetle
FIREBRAT	A small wingless insect
FIVEFOLD	Five times as great
FLATUS	Intestinal gas
FLUBDUB	Pretentious nonsense
FOGDOG	A faint fog
FOU	Drunk
FRIGHTED	Frightened

G

GADZOOKS	A mild oath
GECKO	A tropical lizard
GHOSTY	Ghostly
GIZMO	A gadget
GLEEK	To make a funny remark
GRIPT	Past tense of *grip*

H

HAGBORN	Born of a witch
HOICK	To rapidly change directions
HONDA	Part of a lariat
HOODIE	A gray crow of Europe
HOOCH	Cheap whiskey
HOWDAH	An elephant saddle
HUIC	A call used to encourage hunting hounds
HUSHFUL	Quiet

I

IBEX	A wild goat
IKEBANA	The Japanese art of flower arranging
INEDITA	Unpublished literary works
INVERITY	A lack of truth
IRONNESS	The state of being iron
IXODID	A bloodsucking insect

J

JAPAN	To coat with black lacquer
JAYVEE	A junior varsity athlete
JEHU	A fast driver
JETPORT	A type of airport
JEWFISH	A large marine fish
JIGSAWN	Cut on a jigsaw
JNANA	Knowledge acquired by meditation
JUGHEAD	A dolt

K

KAKA	A New Zealand parrot
KAT	An Arab shrub used as a stimulant
KLONG	An Asian canal
KNEEPAN	The kneecap
KREMLIN	A Russian fortress
KUCHEN	Coffee cake

L

LANDSLID Past tense of *landslide*
LICKSPIT A fawning person
LOCOMOTE To move about
LONGSOME Tediously long
LOSTNESS The state of being lost

LOTTED Distributed fairly
LUNARIAN A supposed inhabitant of the moon
LUNGI A loincloth worn by men of India

M

MAAR A volcanic crater
MAHOUT An elephant keeper
MALEDICT To curse
MEDICO A doctor
MENSA The grinding surface of a tooth

MISLIKER One who mislikes
MOLY A wild garlic
MUDROOM A room for shedding muddy clothing
MUTCH A close-fitting cap

N

NAPOLEON A cream pastry
NGWEE A Zambian unit of currency
NIDERING A coward
NONGREEN Not green
NONSKED An airline without scheduled flying times

NOVERCAL Pertaining to a stepmother
NOYADE Execution by drowning

O

OCTUPLY To eight times the degree
ODDISH Somewhat odd
OLDWIFE A marine fish
ONCES Several single times
ORATRIX A female orator

OUTCHIDE To surpass in chiding
OUTGNAW To surpass in gnawing
OUTWRIT Written better than
OVERSUP To eat to excess

P

PERHAPSES Things open to doubt or conjecture
PIGBOAT A submarine
PLUGUGLY A hoodlum
POETLESS Lacking a poet

PREFAB To construct beforehand
PSST A sound made to get someone's attention
PUNKIN A pumpkin

Q

QIVIUT The wool of a musk ox
QUETZAL A Central American tropical bird

QUITRENT A type of fixed rent due from a tenant

R

RATATAT A quick sharp rapping sound

RAWBONED Having little flesh

REDBONE A hunting dog

ROCKABY A song used to lull a baby to sleep

ROSARIAN A cultivator of roses

ROUGHLEG A large hawk

S

SEEDTIME The season for sowing seeds

SEMIHOBO A person having some of the characteristics of a hobo

SLURBAN Pertaining to a poorly planned suburban area

SOMEWISE Somehow

SQUUSH To squash

SUBECHO An inferior echo

SUBTUNIC A tunic worn below another tunic

SUNSUIT An outfit worn for sunbathing

T

TAMELESS Not capable of being tamed

TANKA A Japanese verse form

TENIASIS Infestation with tapeworms

TENTY Watchful

TEXASES The uppermost structures on a steamboat

TIMPANI Kettledrums

TOLBOOTH A prison

TSUNAMI A very large ocean wave

TURFSKI A specialized type of short ski

TWIGGEN Made of twigs

U

UBIQUE Everywhere

UGSOME Disgusting

ULVA An edible seaweed

UNCAKE To break up a cake

UNHANG To detach from a hanging position

UNRENT Not torn

USQUE Scotch whiskey

V

VANMAN A person who drives a van

VEGETIST One that eats only plant products

VOGIE Vain

VROOM To run an engine at high speed

VUG A small cavity in a mineshaft

W

WAGTAIL A songbird
WASTELOT A vacant lot
WAUGH Damp
WHANG To beat with a whip

WILCO A telecommunications term used to express acknowledgment
WINESOP Food soaked in wine
WRANGS A variant of *wrongs*

X

XERUS An African ground squirrel

XYSTI Roofed areas in ancient Greece used as gymnasiums

Y

YARDWAND A measuring stick
YOKEMATE A companion in work

YOUTHEN To make youthful
YTTRIA A chemical compound

Z

ZANIES Several zany people
ZEBRASS The offspring of a zebra and an ass

ZINGARA A female gypsy
ZONKED Under the influence of a drug

TWO-TO-MAKE-THREE LIST

The following list is one of the first that an aspiring Scrabble® player should learn. There are many times when a play requires hooking on to a two-letter word. If you know the following list, you will get far more mileage from your good letters because you will be able to play them.

Remember how important it was to know the two-letter words? Very much the same thing here.

FRONT HOOKS	The Base Two-Letter Word	BACK HOOKS
These letters can be added to the front of the two-letter word to make a new three-letter word		These letters can be added to the back of the two-letter word to make a new three-letter word

	B	AA	H, L, S
	B, C, D, F, G, H, L, M, P, R, S, T, W	AD	D, O, S, Z
	G, H, K, M, N, S, T, W	AE	None
	A, B, D, H, P, R, Y	AH	A
	None	AI	D, L, M, N, R, S, T
	C, D, G, H, J, L, P, R, T, Y	AM	A, I, P, U
	B, C, F, G, M, P, R, T, V, W	AN	A, D, E, I, T, Y
	B, C, E, F, G, J, L, M, O, P, T, W, Y	AR	C, E, F, K, M, S, T
	A, B, F, G, H, K, L, M, P, R, T, V, W	AS	H, K, P, S
	B, C, E, F, G, H, K, L, M, O, P, R, S, T, V, W	AT	E
	C, D, H, J, L, M, P, R, S, T, V, W, Y	AW	A, E, L, N
	F, L, P, R, S, T, W, Z	AX	E
	B, C, D, F, G, H, J, K, L, M, N, P, R, S, W, Y	AY	E, S
	A	BA	A, D, G, H, L, N, R, S, T, Y
	O	BE	D, E, G, L, N, T, Y
	O	BI	B, D, G, N, O, S, T
	A	BO	A, B, D, G, O, P, S, T, W, X, Y
	A	BY	E, S
	None	DA	B, D, G, H, K, M, P, W, Y
	O	DE	B, E, I, L, N, S, V, W, X, Y
	A, U	DO	C, E, G, L, M, N, R, S, T, W
	K, R	EF	F, S, T
	Y	EH	None
	B, D, E, G, M, S	EL	D, F, K, L, M, S
	G, H, M, R	EM	E, S, U
	B, D, F, H, K, M, P, S, T, W, Y	EN	D, G, S
	F, H, P, S	ER	A, E, G, N, R, S
	D, H, P, R, Y	ES	S

B, F, G, H, J, L, M, N, P, R, S, V, W, Y	ET	A, H
D, H, K, L, R, S, V	EX	None
None	FA	D, G, N, R, S, T, X, Y
A, E	GO	A, B, D, O, R, T, X, Y
A, W	HA	D, E, G, H, J, M, P, S, T, W, Y
S, T	HE	M, N, P, R, S, T, W, X, Y
C, G, K, P	HI	C, D, E, M, N, P, S, T
M, O, R, T, W	HO	B, D, E, G, P, T, W, Y
A, B, D, F, G, H, K, L, M, R, Y	ID	S
K	IF	S
A, B, D, F, G, H, J, K, L, P, R, S, T, V, W, Y	IN	K, N, S
A, B, H, L, M, P, S, T, V, W, X	IS	M
A, B, D, F, G, H, K, L, N, P, S, T, U, W	IT	S
None	JO	B, E, G, T, W, Y
O	KA	B, E, S, T, Y
A	LA	B, C, D, G, M, P, R, S, T, W, X, Y
None	LI	B, D, E, N, P, S, T
None	LO	B, G, O, P, T, W, X
A	MA	C, D, E, G, N, P, R, S, T, W, Y
E	ME	L, M, N, T, W
A	MI	B, D, G, L, M, R, S, X
A, E	MU	D, G, M, N, S, T
None	MY	None
A	NA	B, E, G, T, Y
None	NO	B, D, G, H, M, O, R, S, T, W
G	NU	B, N, S, T
B, C, G, H, M, N, P, R, S, T, Y	OD	D, E, S
D, F, H, J, R, T, V, W	OE	S
None	OF	F, T
F, N, O, P	OH	M, O, S
D, M, N, T, Y	OM	S
C, D, E, F, I, M, S, T, V, W, Y	ON	E, S

		Prefix	Letters
B, C, F, H, K, L, M, P, S, T, W		OP	E, S, T
D, F, G, K, M, N, T		OR	A, B, C, E, S, T
B, C, D, K, N, S, W		OS	E
B, C, D, H, J, L, M, N, P, R, S, T, V, W, Y		OW	E, L, N
B, C, F, G, L, P, S, V		OX	Y
B, C, F, G, H, J, S, T		OY	None
S		PA	C, D, H, L, M, N, P, R, S, T, W, X, Y
		PE	A, D, E, G, N, P, R, S, T, W
A, O		PI	A, C, E, G, N, P, S, T, U, X
None		RE	B, C, D, E, F, I, M, P, S, T, V, X
A, E, I, O		SH	E, H, Y
A		SI	B, C, M, N, P, R, S, T, X
P		SO	B, D, L, N, P, S, T, U, W, X, Y
None		TA	B, D, E, G, J, M, N, O, P, R, S, T, U, V, W, X
E, U		TI	C, E, L, N, P, S, T
		TO	D, E, G, M, N, O, P, R, T, W, Y
None		UN	S
None		UP	O, S
B, D, F, G, H, J, M, N, P, R, S, T		US	E
C, D, H, P, S, T, Y		UT	A, S
B, J, M, N, P		WE	B, D, E, N, T
B, C, G, H, J, M, N, O, P, R, T		WO	E, K, N, O, P, S, T, W
A, E, O		XI	S
T		XU	None
None		YA	H, K, M, P, R, W, Y
None		YE	A, H, N, P, S, T, W
P, R			
A, B, D, E, L, P, R, T, W			

THE 100 MOST COMMON SEVEN-LETTER BINGOS

Finding bingos will become much easier as you gain experience. Playing Scrabble® will give you practice at finding words and it will also help you recognize certain letter groups. The following is a list of the one hundred most commonly held bingos. If you study this list, you will become attuned to the fact that AENORST has not one, not two, but three bingos. These are TREASON, ATONERS, and SENATOR.

If you did not know this, you might overlook these bingos in the heat of battle.

Note that many of the bingo words in this list are obscure. If you read the list a few times, they will become less obscure. And if you read it a few more times, they will become like old friends, and you will recognize and then play them. This is one of the nice things about Scrabble®. It is exactly as challenging as you wish it to be.

The Seven Letters	The Bingos		
AADEINR	ARANEID	ADEINST	DESTAIN, DETAINS, INSTEAD, SAINTED, STAINED
AADEIRT	RADIATE, TIARAED		
AAEEINT	TAENIAE	ADEINTU	AUDIENT
AAEILNO	AEOLIAN	ADEIRST	ARIDEST, ASTRIDE, DIASTER, DISRATE, STAIDER, TARDIES, TIRADES
AAEINST	ENTASIA, TAENIAS		
AAEIRST	ARISTAE, ASTERIA, ATRESIA		
ACEINOT	ACONITE	ADELNOR	LADRONE
ACEIORT	EROTICA	ADELNOT	TALONED
ADEEILN	ALIENED, DELAINE	ADELORT	DELATOR, LEOTARD
ADEEILR	LEADIER	ADENORU	RONDEAU
ADEEINS	ANISEED	ADENOST	DONATES
ADEEIRS	DEARIES, READIES	ADEORST	ROASTED, TORSADE
ADEEIST	IDEATES	ADEORTU	OUTDARE, OUTREAD, READOUT
ADEIINR	DENARII		
ADEIINT	INEDITA	AEEGINR	REGINAE
ADEILOR	DARIOLE	AEEILNR	ALIENER
ADEILOS	ISOLEAD	AEEILNT	LINEATE
ADEILRT	DILATER, TRAILED	AEEILRS	REALISE
ADEINOR	ANEROID	AEEILRT	ATELIER
ADEINRT	DETRAIN, TRAINED	AEEINRT	RETINAE, TRAINEE
ADEIOST	IODATES, TOADIES	AEEINST	ETESIAN
ADEINRS	RANDIES, SANDIER	AEEIRST	AERIEST, SERIATE
ADEINRU	UNAIRED, URANIDE	AEELNRT	ENTERAL, ETERNAL, TELERAN

224

AEENORS	ARENOSE	**AEINRST**	ANESTRI, NASTIER, RATINES, RETAINS, RETINAS, RETSINA, STAINER, STEARIN
AEENRST	EARNEST, EASTERN, NEAREST		
AEEORST	ROSEATE	**AEINRTT**	INTREAT, ITERANT, NATTIER, NITRATE, TERTIAN
AEGINOS	AGONIES, AGONISE		
AEGINRT	GRANITE, INGRATE, TANGIER, TEARING	**AEINRTU**	RUINATE, TAURINE, URANITE, URINATE
AEGNORT	NEGATOR	**AEINSTU**	AUNTIES, SINUATE
AEIILNR	AIRLINE	**AELNORS**	LOANERS, RELOANS
AEIINRS	SENARII	**AELNORU**	ALEURON
AEIINRT	INERTIA	**AELNOST**	TOLANES
AEIINST	ISATINE	**AELORTU**	TORULAE
AEIIRST	AIRIEST	**AENORST**	ATONERS, SENATOR, TREASON
AEILNOR	AILERON, ALIENOR		
AEILNOS	ANISOLE	**AENORSU**	ARENOUS
AEILNOT	ELATION, TOENAIL	**AENOSTU**	SOUTANE
AEILNRS	ALIENERS, NAILERS	**AINORST**	AROINTS, RATIONS
AEILNRT	LATRINE, RATLINE, RELIANT, RETINAL, TRENAIL	**AINORTU**	RAINOUT
		DEIINOT	EDITION
AEILNST	ELASTIN, ENTAILS, NAILSET, SALIENT, SALTINE, TENAILS	**DEIIORT**	DIORITE
		DEILNOT	LENTOID
		DEINORS	DINEROS, INDORSE, ORDINES, ROSINED, SORDINE
AEILNUT	ALUNITE		
AEILOST	ISOLATE	**DEINORU**	DOURINE, NEUROID
AEILRST	REALIST, RETAILS, SALTIER, SALTIRE, SLATIER, TAILERS	**DEIORST**	EDITORS, SORTIED, STEROID, STORIED, TRIODES
AEILRTU	URALITE	**DEIORTU**	OUTRIDE
AEIMNOR	MORAINE, ROMAINE	**EEINRST**	ENTIRES, ENTRIES, TRIENES
AEIMNOT	AMNIOTE		
AEINNOT	ENATION	**EEILNOR**	ELOINER
AEINNRT	ENTRAIN	**EEINRTU**	RETINUE, REUNITE, UTERINE
AEINORS	ERASION		
AEINOST	ATONIES	**EGINORT**	GENITOR
AEINRRT	RETRAIN, TERRAIN, TRAINER	**EIINORS**	IRONIES, NOISIER

EIINOST	INOSITE	**EINORST**	OESTRIN, NORITES, STONIER, ORIENTS
EILNORS	NEROLIS		
EILNORT	RETINOL	**EINORTU**	ROUTINE

THE 50 MOST COMMON EIGHT-LETTER BINGOS

There will be occasional moments when you feel that you have a good play, but you just can't quite find it. It may be that your best play is an eight-letter bingo that uses a letter on the board plus the ones in your rack.

The following list could provide the answer for you. It includes, in alphabetical order, the most frequent eight-letter bingo groups, plus all the available bingos in each group.

The real importance of this list is not that you can find all the eight-letter anagrams. The important thing is that you do look for eight- (or even nine-) letter bingos when appropriate.

The Eight Letters	**The Bingos**		
AADEEIRT	ERADIATE	**ADEGINOR**	ORGANDIE
AAEEILNT	ALIENATE	**ADEIINOT**	IDEATION, IODINATE
AAEINORT	AERATION	**ADEIINRT**	DAINTIER
AAEINRST	ANTISERA, RATANIES, SEATRAIN	**ADEILNOT**	DELATION
		ADEILORT	IDOLATER, TAILORED
ABEINORT	BARITONE, OBTAINER, REOBTAIN, TABORINE	**ADEINORS**	ANEROIDS
ACEINORT	ANORETIC, CREATION, REACTION	**ADEINORT**	AROINTED, ORDINATE, RATIONED
ADEEILNT	DATELINE, ENTAILED, LINEATED	**ADEINOST**	ASTONIED, SEDATION
		ADEINRST	STRAINED, DETRAINS
ADEEILRT	DETAILER, ELATERID, RETAILED	**ADEINRTU**	INDURATE, RUINATED, URINATED
ADEEINRS	ARSENIDE	**ADEIORST**	ASTEROID
ADEEINRT	DETAINER, RETAINED	**AEEIINRT**	INERTIAE
ADEEINST	ANDESITE	**AEEILNRS**	ALIENERS
ADEEIRST	READIEST, SERIATED, STEADIER	**AEEILNRT**	ELATERIN, ENTAILER, TREENAIL

AEEILORT	AEROLITE	**AEILNOST**	ELATIONS, INSOLATE, TOENAILS
AEEILRST	ATELIERS, EARLIEST, LEARIEST, REALTIES	**AEILNRST**	ENTRAILS, LATRINES, RATLINES, RETINALS, TRENAILS
AEEINRST	ARSENITE, RESINATE, STEARINE, TRAINEES		
		AEILNRTU	AUNTLIER, RETINULA, TENURIAL
AEEINRSU	UNEASIER		
AEENORST	EARSTONE, RESONATE	**AEINNORT**	ANOINTER, REANOINT
AEGILNOR	GERANIOL, REGIONAL	**AEINOPRT**	ATROPINE
AEGILNOT	GELATION, LEGATION	**AEINORRT**	ANTERIOR
AEGINORS	ORGANISE	**AEINORST**	NOTARIES, SENORITA
AEHINORT	ANTIHERO	**AEINRSTU**	RUINATES, TAURINES, URANITES, URINATES
AEIILNRT	INERTIAL		
AEIINRST	INERTIAS, RAINIEST	**AEIORSTU**	OUTRAISE, SAUTOIRE
AEILNORS	AILERONS, ALIENORS	**DEEINORT**	ORIENTED
AEILNORT	ORIENTAL, RELATION	**EEINORST**	ONERIEST, SEROTINE

THE "SATIRE" AND OTHER LISTS

The following lists are very useful aids to finding bingos. Each list consists of a key six-letter group, plus the effect of adding each letter of the alphabet to it.

For example: If you see your rack has SATIRE, and if your seventh letter is an F, you will know automatically that you have FAIREST and you will know it is the only bingo.

If your rack is SATIRE plus a K, you will know automatically that there is no bingo, no matter how hard you look.

This section includes ten key six-letter groups. They are well worth reviewing.

KEY SIX-LETTER WORDS

AEIRST—SATIRE

A ARISTAE, ASTERIA, ATRESIA

B BAITERS, BARITES, REBAITS, TERBIAS

C CRISTAE, RACIEST, STEARIC

D ARIDEST, ASTRIDE, DIASTER, DISRATE, STAIDER, TARDIES, TIRADES

E AERIEST, SERIATE

F	FAIREST	**P**	PANTIES, PATINES, SAPIENT, SPINATE
G	AIGRETS, GAITERS, SEAGIRT, STAGIER, TRIAGES	**Q**	None
H	HASTIER	**R**	ANESTRI, NASTIER, RATINES, RETAINS, RETINAS, RETSINA, STAINER, STEARIN
I	AIRIEST	**S**	ENTASIS, SESTINA, TANSIES, TISANES
J	None	**T**	INSTATE, SATINET
K	None	**U**	AUNTIES, SINUATE
L	REALIST, RETAILS, SALTIER, SALTIRE, SLATIER, TAILERS	**V**	NAIVEST, NATIVES, VAINEST
M	IMARETS, MAESTRI, MISRATE, SMARTIE	**W**	TAWNIES, WANIEST
N	ANESTRI, NASTIER, RATINES, RETAINS, RETINAS, RETSINA, STAINER, STEARIN	**X**	SEXTAIN
O	None	**Y**	None
P	PARTIES, PASTIER, PIASTER, PIASTRE, PIRATES, TRAIPSE	**Z**	ZANIEST, ZEATINS

F FAIREST
G AIGRETS, GAITERS, SEAGIRT, STAGIER, TRIAGES
H HASTIER
I AIRIEST
J None
K None
L REALIST, RETAILS, SALTIER, SALTIRE, SLATIER, TAILERS
M IMARETS, MAESTRI, MISRATE, SMARTIE
N ANESTRI, NASTIER, RATINES, RETAINS, RETINAS, RETSINA, STAINER, STEARIN
O None
P PARTIES, PASTIER, PIASTER, PIASTRE, PIRATES, TRAIPSE
Q None
R TARRIES, TARSIER
S SATIRES
T ARTIEST, ARTISTE, ATTIRES, IRATEST, RATITES, STRIATE, TASTIER
U None
V VASTIER, VERITAS
W WAISTER, WAITERS, WARIEST, WASTRIE
X None
Y None
Z None

AEINST—SATINE

A ENTASIA, TAENIAS
B BASINET
C CINEAST
D DESTAIN, DETAINS, INSTEAD, SAINTED, STAINED
E ETESIAN
F FAINEST
G EASTING, EATINGS, INGATES, INGESTA, SEATING, TEASING
H SHEITAN, STHENIA
I ISATINE
J None
K INTAKES
L ELASTIN, ENTAILS, NAILSET, SALIENT, SALTINE, TENAILS
M ETAMINS, INMATES, TAMEINS
N INANEST
O ATONIES

P PANTIES, PATINES, SAPIENT, SPINATE
Q None
R ANESTRI, NASTIER, RATINES, RETAINS, RETINAS, RETSINA, STAINER, STEARIN
S ENTASIS, SESTINA, TANSIES, TISANES
T INSTATE, SATINET
U AUNTIES, SINUATE
V NAIVEST, NATIVES, VAINEST
W TAWNIES, WANIEST
X SEXTAIN
Y None
Z ZANIEST, ZEATINS

AEINRT—RETINA

A None
B None
C CERATIN, CERTAIN, CREATIN
D DETRAIN, TRAINED
E RETINAE, TRAINEE
F FAINTER
G GRANITE, INGRATE, TANGIER, TEARING
H INEARTH
I INERTIA
J None
K KERATIN
L LATRINE, RATLINE, RELIANT, RETINAL, TRENAIL
M MINARET, RAIMENT
N ENTRAIN
O None
P PAINTER, PERTAIN, REPAINT
Q None
R RETRAIN, TERRAIN, TRAINER
S ANESTRI, NASTIER, RATINES, RETAINS, RETINAS, RETSINA, STAINER, STEARIN
T INTREAT, ITERANT, NATTIER, NITRATE, TERTIAN
U RUINATE, TAURINE, URANITE, URINATE
V None
W TAWNIER, TINWEAR
X None
Y None
Z None

AENRST—SANTER

A None
B BANTERS
C CANTERS, NECTARS, RECANTS, SCANTER, TANRECS, TRANCES
D STANDER
E EARNEST, EASTERN, NEAREST
F None
G ARGENTS, GARNETS, STRANGE
H ANTHERS, THENARS
I ANESTRI, NASTIER, RATINES, RETAINS, RETINAS, RETSINA, STAINER, STEARIN
J None
K RANKEST, TANKERS
L ANTLERS, RENTALS, SALTERN, STERNAL
M MARTENS, SARMENT, SMARTEN
N TANNERS
O ATONERS, SENATOR, TREASON
P ARPENTS, ENTRAPS, PARENTS, PASTERN, TREPANS
Q None
R ERRANTS, RANTERS
S None
T NATTERS, RATTENS
U NATURES, SAUNTER
V SERVANT, TAVERNS, VERSANT
W WANTERS
X None
Y None
Z None

AEINRS—SARINE

A None
B None
C ARSENIC, CARNIES
D RANDIES, SANDIER, SARDINE
E None
F INFARES
G EARINGS, ERASING, GAINERS, REAGINS, REGAINS, REGINAS, SEARING, SERINGA
H HERNIAS
I SENARII
J None
K SNAKIER
L ALINERS, NAILERS

M MARINES, REMAINS, SEMINAR
N INSANER, INSNARE
O ERASION
P PANIERS, RAPINES
Q None
R SIERRAN
S ARSINES
T ANESTRI, NASTIER, RATINES, RETAINS, RETINAS, RETSINA, STAINER, STEARIN
U None
V RAVINES
W None
X None
Y None
Z None

AEERST—RESEAT

A AERATES
B BEATERS, BERATES, REBATES
C CERATES, CREATES, ECARTES
D DEAREST, REDATES, SEDATER
E None
F AFREETS, FEASTER
G ERGATES, RESTAGE
H AETHERS, HEATERS, REHEATS
I SERIATE, AERIEST
J None
K RETAKES
L ELATERS, REALEST, RELATES, STEALER
M STEAMER
N EARNEST, EASTERN, NEAREST
O ROSEATE
P REPEATS
Q None
R SERRATE, TEARERS
S RESEATS, SEAREST, TEASERS, TESSERA, EASTERS, SEATERS
T ESTREAT, RESTATE, RETASTE
U AUSTERE
V None
W SWEATER
X None
Y None
Z None

AEILST—SEALIT

A None

B ALBITES, BASTILE, BESTIAL, BLASTIE, STABILE
C ELASTIC, LACIEST, LATICES
D DETAILS, DILATES
E None
F FETIALS
G AIGLETS, LIGATES
H HALITES, HELIAST
I LAITIES
J None
K LAKIEST, TALKIES
L TAILLES, TALLIES
M None
N ELASTIN, ENTAILS, NAILSET, SALIENT, SALTINE, TENAILS
O ISOLATE
P APLITES, PALIEST, PLATIES, TALIPES
Q None
R REALIST, RETAILS, SALTIER, SALTIRE, SLATIER, TAILERS
S SALTIES
T None
U None
V ESTIVAL
W None
X None
Y None
Z LAZIEST

EENRST—ENTERS

A EARNEST, EASTERN, NEAREST
B None
C CENTERS, CENTRES, TENRECS
D TENDERS
E ENTREES, RETENES, TEENERS
F None
G GERENTS, REGENTS
H None
I ENTIRES, ENTRIES, TRIENES
J None
K None
L NESTLER, RELENTS
M None
N RENNETS, TENNERS
O ESTRONE
P PENSTER, PRESENT, REPENTS, SERPENT
Q None
R RENTERS, STERNER

S NESTERS, RESENTS
T NETTERS, TENTERS
U NEUTERS, RETUNES, TENURES, TUREENS
V VENTERS
W WESTERN
X EXTERNS
Y STYRENE, YESTERN
Z None

AEILRT—TAILER

A None
B TRIABLE, LIBRATE
C ARTICLE, RECITAL
D DILATER, TRAILED
E ATELIER
F None
G None
H LATHIER
I None
J None
K RATLIKE, TALKIER
L LITERAL, TALLIER
M MALTIER, MARLITE
N LATRINE, RATLINE, RELIANT, RETINAL, TRENAIL
O None
P PLAITER, PLATIER
Q None
R RETRIAL, TRAILER
S REALIST, RETAILS, SALTIER, SALTIRE, SLATIER, TAILERS
T TERTIAL
U URALITE
V None
W None
X None
Y IRATELY, REALITY, TEARILY
Z None

ADEIRS—SADIRE

A None
B ABIDERS, BRAISED, DARBIES, SEABIRD
C RADICES, SIDECAR
D None
E DEARIES, READIES
F None
G None

H	DASHIER, HARDIES, SHADIER	R	RAIDERS
I	DAIRIES, DIARIES	S	None
J	None	T	ARIDEST, ASTRIDE, DIASTER,
K	DAIKERS, DARKIES		DISRATE, STAIDER, TARDIES,
L	DERAILS, DIALERS		TIRADES
M	MISREAD, ADMIRES,	U	RESIDUA
	SEDARIM, SIDEARM	V	ADVISER
N	RANDIES, SANDIER, SARDINE	W	None
O	None	X	RADIXES
P	ASPIRED, DESPAIR, DIAPERS,	Y	None
	PRAISED	Z	None
Q	None		

IMPROVING YOUR GAME

If you have read this far into the book, it means (we hope) that you have been hooked. If so, the hints offered here will be a big help, because you will be inclined to use them.

Things you can do include:

1. Join a Scrabble® Club. Selchow & Righter has licensed hundreds of these across the country. Any new player will be welcomed, introduced to the club, and games will be arranged. These clubs are excellent places to meet other Scrabble® players and to learn the game. For information, write:

    > SCRABBLE® CROSSWORD GAME PLAYERS, INC.
    > Box 700, Front Street Garden
    > Greenport, NY 11944
    >
    > (516) 477-0033

2. When possible, play better players. In almost any kind of competition, it is harder to be better than the best person around you. If you don't play better players, you don't improve.

3. Play solitaire games. These are good because you can refer freely to the dictionary and various word lists. This makes these games excellent learning experiences. You can measure your progress by keeping track of the total points scored by you and your "opponent." One nice thing about this form of Scrabble® is that you always win!

4. Read the available literature. All of the following materials are highly recommended.
    a. *The Scrabble® Players' Newsletter.* This is published every two months by Selchow & Righter. It covers all aspects of Scrabble® and addresses itself to experts and new players alike. It includes quizzes and also complete tournament information, plus results. For information, write:

        > SCRABBLE® CROSSWORD GAME PLAYERS, INC.
        > Box 700, Front Street Garden
        > Greenport, NY 11944

b. *A Champion's Guide to Winning Scrabble®*, by Joel Wapnick, published by Stein & Day. This book emphasizes expert situations but still has lots for new players. The many problems and diagrams will challenge anyone. Included in this book are the author's experiences in the Scrabble® world. A nice personal touch.

5. Study word lists. In addition to the ten word lists offered in this section, there are many other useful lists available. These can be found either at a Scrabble® club or by writing Selchow & Righter.
   This is a good way to improve word awareness, since it can be done at odd moments.
   If you really feel motivated, I would suggest making a tape and listening when appropriate, or making flash cards showing the letter group (alphabetized) on one side and the words on the other.

6. Enter tournaments. Most divide players by ability and they are an enjoyable way to combine travel with meeting new people.

7. Think positively. When the letters are poor, play thoughtfully and not carelessly. Good letters will come. Bad luck is impersonal and will vanish as quickly as it appeared. Be ready when the tide turns.

GOOD LUCK

ABOUT THE AUTHORS

In 1957 **Michael Lawrence** entered U.C. Berkeley with every intention of acquiring a degree in mathematics, but in his first year he discovered bridge, which became his real major. Three years later, bridge completely took his interest and he dropped out of U.C. to pursue it. Since then he has won every U.S. title, some more than once, and has twice won the world championship.

But bridge is not his only foray into the games world. In addition to having written thirteen major books on bridge and earning the title, "bridge author of the 80s," he wrote the bestselling WINNING BACK-GAMMON. He's had fun with Scrabble® since his grandfather first taught him to play, and is now a registered fanatic. THE ULTIMATE GUIDE TO WINNING AT SCRABBLE® with John Ozag is his first joint effort, and he plans to beat Ozag in their next game.

John Ozag has been playing Scrabble® seriously for over twenty years. He was the winner of the first official Scrabble® tournament held in Chicago in 1975 and was a premium competitor in the midwest for many years. He has been a participant at all the national Scrabble® tournaments, and at the 1983 championship he provided the technical commentary. Over the years, he has written a variety of articles for the *Scrabble® Players Newsletter.* He currently lives in the San Francisco area and works as an insurance broker and investment planner. He plans to beat Lawrence in their next Scrabble® game.